PRAISE FOR

Listening Below the Noise

"What a hunger I have for the practice of silence, for a dialing down, for unplugging! This beautiful book is a primer on how to begin, and a glimpse of the deep rewards. Anne LeClaire is the loveliest of teachers."

—Jane Hamilton, author of
A Map of the World and *The Book of Ruth*

"Anne LeClaire takes her reader to that quiet place within where it becomes possible to hear what one's heart needs to say. Her story is made all the more powerful because she practices what she writes."

—Joan Anderson, author of
A Year by the Sea and *A Second Journey*

"LeClaire illuminates the treasures that can be found in the practice of silence. But the book does much, much more. It offers readers the possibility of finding grace and peace in the natural world and in ourselves. Elegant and honest, *Listening Below the Noise* is one of those rare books that finds its way into our hearts, and stays there, working its magic again and again."

—Ann Hood,
author of *The Knitting Circle*

"LeClaire gently leads us out of shallow cultural waters and shows us the art of swimming in an ocean of silence. Her words have a buoyancy that emboldens us to kick our legs, to blow bubbles, and to glide reverently into the great and wondrous unknown."

—Christopher M. Leighton,
Executive Director of the Institute
for Christian & Jewish Studies

"This is a book that heals the soul, a classic like *Gift from the Sea*. It left me spellbound and stunned by its power."

—Luanne Rice, author of
Light of the Moon and *What Matters Most*

"Against the cacophony that pervades our lives, novelist LeClaire (*The Lavender Hour*) offers a persuasive antidote: silence.... LeClaire's prose is colloquial, friendly and familiar, and the book is as much memoir as it is inspiration."

—*Publishers Weekly*

"Luminous."

—*The NewsHour with Jim Lehrer*

"Eloquent and moving.... Although technically a memoir, this book moves beyond that genre into spirituality and philosophy. LeClaire's reputation as a novelist may draw readers to this lovely book, which should also have crossover appeal to spiritual seekers of any religion and no religion."

—*Booklist*

"Fascinating . . . driven by marvelous writing throughout. . . . A vivid and significant book full of insights and inspiration."

—*Reader's Digest*

"LeClaire leads us gently and persuasively through her inspirational experience."

—Carole Goldberg, *Hartford Courant*

"A quietly effective and beautiful book."   —*Cape Women*

"Engaging. . . . Poetic and intimate. . . . A refreshing and important book for an age in which people increasingly tend to avoid silence, continually tuning in to noise and information."   —*The Rumpus*

CHRISTOPHER D. LeCLAIRE

ABOUT THE AUTHOR

ANNE D. LeCLAIRE is a former reporter, radio news broadcaster, and op-ed columnist whose work has appeared in *Redbook,* the *Boston Sunday Globe,* and the *New York Times,* among other publications. She is the author of eight novels, and translations of her work have been published in twenty-four countries. She lives on Cape Cod. Visit her website at www.anneleclaire.com.

CHRISTOPHER D. LECLAIRE

ABOUT THE PHOTOGRAPHER

CHRISTOPHER D. LECLAIRE, the author's son, is a published author, visual artist, and commercial fisherman whose photography has been exhibited in galleries on Cape Cod and in Boston and Delaware. He lives on Cape Cod.

Listening Below the Noise

Also by Anne D. LeClaire

FICTION

THE TRANSFORMATIVE POWER OF SILENCE

Listening BELOW
THE *Noise*

ANNE D. LeCLAIRE

PHOTOGRAPHY BY CHRISTOPHER LeCLAIRE

HARPER PERENNIAL

NEW YORK • LONDON • TORONTO • SYDNEY • NEW DELHI • AUCKLAND

HARPER PERENNIAL

A hardcover edition of this book was published in 2009 by Harper, an imprint of HarperCollins Publishers.

HarperCollins books may be purchased for educational, business, or sales promotional use. For information please write: Special Markets Department, HarperCollins Publishers, 10 East 53rd Street, New York, NY 10022.

FIRST HARPER PERENNIAL EDITION PUBLISHED 2010.

Designed by Leah Carlson-Stanisic

Library of Congress Cataloging-in-Publication Data is available upon request.

ISBN 978-0-06-135336-9

10 11 12 13 14   OV/RRD   10 9 8 7 6 5 4 3 2 1

For Deborah Schneider

Contents

"Silence was the food I was after."

May Sarton, *Plant Dreaming Deep*

INTRODUCTION

The Secret Garden

WHEN I WAS A GIRL, my favorite book was *The Secret Garden*. I received the Frances Hodgson Burnett classic the Christmas I was ten, and each night that winter I curled up on the sofa to lose myself in the story of young Mary Lennox. Although she was described as an unwanted, lonely, and slightly unpleasant child, she captured my heart and imagination from the opening pages. I wept when her parents died in a cholera epidemic in India and worried for her when she was shipped off to an uncle's estate in England. Her discovery of a hidden door that opened to a secluded garden completely enchanted me, and I thrilled as, within its walls, she was transformed from a yellow-faced, sickly child to a hearty and adventuresome girl.

After I finished the book, I became consumed to near obsession with the idea of finding such a mysterious and beautiful place hidden from ordinary sight by an ivied wall and iron gate, a magical spot that would belong only to me. On the rural farm where we lived such a possibility seemed remote, but whenever I visited my grandparents in Boston and explored the city with my grandfather, I would search for concealed gates in brick walls.

Introduction

The idea of a cloistered place, happened upon quite by accident, holds appeal, whatever our age. The hidden key, the locked gate, and the idea of a sacred space are constants in mythology and are archetypal metaphors that lie at the heart of most spiritual traditions. But as I grew into adulthood, I stopped looking for such things. I became, perhaps not unlike you, too overwhelmed with juggling my life to contemplate such childlike fantasies of escape. My days were occupied with obligations and mundane responsibilities: grocery shopping, cooking, dentist appointments, committee meetings, book deadlines, correspondence, banking, and all the routine maintenance of car, house, yard, body, and especially relationships with family and friends. The list seemed unending. Like too many of us, I mistook a busy life for a rich one.

And then in midlife, and quite unexpectedly, I discovered my own hidden garden.

Seventeen years ago, on a January afternoon in 1992, I stopped. Simply that.

I set aside one day for silence and for twenty-four hours I did not speak. At that time I had no idea this would be the beginning of a personal odyssey of exploration and discovery, a long journey not without difficulties but one that, in the ensuing years, would transform my life. Nor did

Introduction

I imagine that, like young Mary Lennox, I would come to discover the healing and transformative powers of a sacred space. That day I only opened a gate, stood at a threshold, and took one step. Like the beginning of all mythic journeys, this was enough.

This is the story of my secret garden, begun on that distant winter day on Cape Cod on the shores of Nantucket Sound.

I hope something in it will whisper to you. Perhaps, if you are moved to stop, you too will awaken to the benefits and pleasures of a world that is waiting beneath the noise.

PART ONE

Entry

CHAPTER 1

Eiders

Hearing THE *Call*

A SONGBIRD LED MARY LENNOX to the hidden garden at her uncle's country estate and unearthed the key that would open the gate. But it had been there all along, waiting for her.

Are there certain sanctuaries to which you are drawn for inspiration and restoration, for solace or consolation? The mountains, the seashore? A chapel? Even a coffee shop on the corner? My own is a narrow swath at the edge of Nantucket Sound on the south side of Cape Cod, a place I often look to for grounding because the steady rhythm of waves, the briny air, the call of gulls, and the give of sand beneath my feet have a way of anchoring me and easing confusion. And so on this particular January afternoon, in need of comfort, I headed there.

Earlier that morning, my friend Margaret had called from the hospital to tell me her mother was dying. Preoccupied with concern and sadness, I wrestled with the hard knowledge that there was nothing I could do to safeguard my friend from pain. I could neither control life nor delay death and hated feeling so helpless. A few years earlier, both my father and my beloved mother-in-law had died, and I still had days when, in the supermarket or at the garage waiting for an oil change, I suddenly would be swept with grief. Now, triggered by Margaret's situation, memories of these losses overtook me. Much later I would wonder: Was it my very vulnerability in that moment that made me receptive to what followed? Is this cracking open one of the unforeseen gifts of sorrow?

The ebb tide was at midpoint, leaving a narrow wrack line of seaweed and shells and the detritus we humans trail in our wake—plastic bottles, a soda can, a chunk of orange Styrofoam from a lobster buoy, and, nestled in the arms of a clump of eelgrass, an empty Bacardi bottle. The sky was cloudless, and the horizon offered no clear delineation between the blue of sky and sea, a sort of blending that can trick the eye and create vertigo for sailors and pilots. The sound, like the sky, was calm. Even in the distance there was no chop. Twenty feet out, a lone harbor seal basked on a partially exposed rock; closer to shore, a pair of black-and-white sea ducks dove for food.

I have learned much about the physical world from my husband, who is a commercial fisherman, hunter, and naturalist. One of the first things Hillary taught me after we married and I moved to Cape Cod was how to identify waterfowl by coloration, habits, and flight. Often, as we walked along the salt marsh and shore near our home, he would point out how the surface feeders—mallards, teals, black ducks—took wing straight up. He said the divers—scoters, canvasbacks, redheads—pattered along the surface when taking off. This day the pair of ducks in the sound were eiders, little engineering marvels that use their wings to swim underwater, sometimes thirty-five to sixty feet below the surface.

I paused to watch as they bobbed like plumed buoys atop the water and then dove to feed, staying under for what seemed like two or three minutes before shooting up again. Hillary had once explained that some birds, like grebes, have more hemoglobin in their blood, and the higher concentrations of oxygen allow them to stay underwater for extended periods. I supposed this was true of eiders, too. I inhaled deeply and tried to hold my breath in concert, but was forced to exhale before they surfaced. Again I tried. And again. Deep breath in, hold, exhale. My lung capacity could not equal theirs, and I was awed at how long they could remain submerged. Years later, Margaret would tell me that as I patterned my breath to the sea ducks, I was practicing *pranayama*, the conscious breathing that is one of the eight stages of Yoga. Such breath work, she explained, actually changes the physiology of the body, preparing one for hard work and readying one for meditation. Was I then, on some level, preparing myself for work I didn't even know awaited me?

As I focused on the eiders my sadness and confusion abated. Although I could neither stay the death of Margaret's mother nor protect my friend from the inevitability of loss, a deep comfort washed over me. Many years earlier, during a troubling time, I'd received a card imprinted with the words of the medieval mystic Lady Julian of Norwich. Now as I stood there, staring out at the sound, they scrolled through my brain: *All will be well and all will be well and all matter of things will be well.*

The phrase echoed in my mind, calming and soothing me, and something I can only describe as reverence slipped in, so hushed I didn't know the exact moment it took me, only that I felt an acute appreciation for the ever-constant cycle of seasons and tides and years, and for natural beauty so compelling it held the power to ease a troubled heart. I was taken with a sensation of timelessness and connection with the universe. To put it simply, in that brief moment on a Cape Cod beach, I was aware both of the glory and the privilege of being alive and of the incredible puniness of my spot in the universe.

.   .   .

This feeling of connecting with something larger than myself stopped me in my tracks. I found myself giving thanks for the splendor of the seashore and the sea ducks playing out life's essentials before me. I was swept with gratitude for the great good fortune that had landed me in this particular place on the planet, and, especially, for the sacred held in ordinary moments like these. I had much to be grateful for on this day: my husband and children, our home, my friends, my health and life's work, my life. Certainly I have also known pain and bone-shifting bereavement—who among us hasn't?—but in that moment I glimpsed and fleetingly understood the necessary and transformative role that suffering, grief, and loss play, how experiencing these allows our hearts to break open to compassion and empathy. I was taken by a profound and pervasive gratitude. Tears welled, and I sent a spontaneous prayer out over the waters, not of petition but of thanksgiving: *I am so blessed. So blessed I don't know what to do.*

. . .

Later, I would barely trust the memory. That short space of urgent gratitude held the first mystical occurrence I had ever consciously experienced. As I stood there beneath the azure sky gazing at the eiders, I actually heard three words, heard them so clearly that I turned my head to search the sands for a sign of someone else. But I was alone on the winter beach. Then I heard them again. "Sit in silence."

For some reason, hearing a disembodied voice did not cause me to panic or to question my stability. Instead, I resumed walking along the shore, as if hearing a voice on a deserted beach was the most natural thing in the world. As I continued along the yielding wet sand, the phrase played across my mind like foam on surf, the cadence nearly hypnotic.

Sit in silence. Sit in silence. Sit in silence.

What did it mean? I'd had no previous experience with any practice of silence—formal or casual. To the contrary, the concept was alien to my personality, like expecting a flamingo to transform herself into a garden vole. In high school, I was once given three detentions in a single study hall because I found it impossible to sit through forty minutes without talking to the girl next to me. To say I was chatty would be an understatement. The person at the movie theater you shush so you can hear the film? That would be me. Stillness was something that cloaked monks and mystics or burdened mutes. What place could it possibly hold in my life?

I turned away from the beach and started walking home. But all the while, the directive persisted. *Sit in silence.* Again I toyed with a possible meaning. Certainly I didn't think I was receiving a great message from the universe. Okay. From *God*, the big guy himself. I would be the last person to expect celestial communications. Although I had enjoyed Sunday school as a child—all those parables and miracles: Joseph and his coat, water turned to wine, Moses hidden in the bulrushes and later parting the Red Sea—I'd stopped attending church with regularity the day I headed off to college, disheartened by a history of wars fought for centuries over religious beliefs and deeply disillusioned by the exclusivity of so many traditions. Since then my attention to religious matters had been sporadic, although after I saw the first *Star Wars* movie I'd dreamed Yoda spoke to me. In the vision he was standing at the end of a path with Buddha and Jesus, who both pretty much ignored me. Which was fine by me. I knew what happened when you started conversing with the likes of them. You ended up putting your furniture in a yard sale, shaving your head, and working with the poor in Calcutta.

No, I didn't think I was being sent messages from heaven. Finally I considered the obvious. Maybe it meant simply what it said. Instantly, almost as a whim but with an accompanying jolt of anticipation and curiosity, I decided to take the words at face value. Starting the next morning, I would not speak for twenty-four hours.

. . .

"You're not going to talk at all?" my husband said.

"For one day," I said.

"Why?" he asked.

I was okay with hearing a disembodied voice, but I wasn't so sure Hillary would think it was a good sign. Who wants to hear that from a partner? "I just need to," I said.

I should tell you something here about Hillary. He is practical, tied to land and sea, a nurturing man who, when one of our children, Hope and Chris, threw up in the middle of the night, was the one who got up and changed the sheets without one complaint while I stumbled around bleary-eyed. He can split and stack a cord of firewood, pilot a jet plane, plot a course, change a spark plug, and cook a prize-winning poached egg. He's generous to a fault and sexy to boot—when we were first dating, just the sight of him in his flight suit made me swoon. Plus he's funny, which is nearly as seductive as the flight-suit thing.

"Hillary is soooo supportive," friends say whenever I head off to teach creative writing in France or Ireland or for a six-week writing sabbatical seven states away, leaving him to deal with the practicalities of our life. Reading between the lines, I hear: *How does he put up with you?*

On the flip side, he's stubborn and doesn't welcome change. Even minor alterations, like rearranged couches and chairs, throw him into a tizzy for days. Our children once gave him a T-shirt with Garfield sliding down the front, leaving scratch marks from collar to waist. It read, "Anything I ever let go of had claw marks all over it." That's Hillary.

So, in a way, I should have expected resistance.

"But what if Hope or Chris calls and wants to talk to you?" he asked.

"I don't know."

"Or what if Margaret's mother dies?"

I paused, my resolve momentarily weakened. Mary's cancer had advanced and her family had been told she had at most forty-eight hours to live. When she passed, I would want to be with Margaret. I immediately felt weighted by the beliefs women have always been taught: we should be available to those we love; our families' needs come before our own.

"Maybe now isn't a good time for this," Hillary said.

"I don't know if there will ever be a good time," I hedged. I don't know how you react in the face of resistance, even one as slight as this, but in the face of opposition—real, projected, or imaginary—I often cave.

"I still don't know why you need to do this," he said.

How could I respond when it wasn't yet clear to me? Why this growing conviction that silence was something I needed to do?

"I'm not sure myself," I surprised myself by saying. "But I'm going to try." Certainly I had no intimation of how profoundly my life was about to change, and in ways I could not anticipate. I was unaware that I was setting out on a deep inner voyage that would lead to a more fulfilling life. I only knew one thing: For a single day I was going to attempt silence. I would not speak.

In the many years following that winter afternoon, I would come to learn that every religious and spiritual tradition has a history of silence, that silence itself is the most fundamental of all spiritual disciplines, with as many ways to observe and cultivate it as there are to pray or bake bread. I would discover that it can be a welcoming, deeply restful space, but also that it can be a trying place that could set my teeth on edge with the need for distraction, raising resistance.

In the coming years, silence—observed both while in community and in solitude—would nourish me. It would serve as a place of restoration and reflection, where I would birth creativity, stretch personal boundaries, and expand awareness. Like others who have traveled the path of stillness I would journey through loneliness to discover unity, through isolation to know connection, through anxiety to find acceptance and surrender. I would experience soul longings and bliss, as well as confusion and fear. Silence was to become a place of deep spiritual work where I would circle out, delve deep, and learn the necessary skill of truly listening—both to others and to myself. It would become my greatest teacher, giving me a center from which to live, testing me, and facilitating healing. It would bring me to myself and make that self stronger.

In such stillness, I would hear the voice of wisdom that can come when sacred space is held open. I would find in this deceptively simple practice the meaning of commitment and attentiveness, the center of soul. Like countless others before me, I would come to silence to learn how to listen. In listening, I would hear.

But I am getting ahead of myself. Back on the eve of the first day, I stepped into silence with little more than curiosity, holding no greater intent than to refrain from speaking for twenty-four hours, to experience for one day what stillness meant.

.   .   .

Morning—first light, really, Hillary lying at my side, already awake.

"I love you," he said.

It felt strange not to respond, and scary, as if I were withholding, keeping a piece of myself apart. Once, as an experiment in mindfulness, I had brushed my teeth with my nondominant hand for three days. As I'd concentrated on this ordinary and automatic act, it felt clumsy and artificial. This new and intentional silence was like that. Everything familiar felt novel and self-conscious. Beneath the blanket, I reached over and squeezed Hillary's hand.

He enfolded my fingers with his. "I know you do," he said. Our eyes met. How many times over the years had we woken and exchanged words of love? Certainly thousands.

But as we lay in early-morning light, holding hands and surrounded by stillness, we shared an intimacy that felt new. The night before, I had wondered—actually feared—if cut off from speech I would feel isolated. Now, lying next to Hillary, I felt especially connected to him, a bond that seemed nearly holy. I thought about how automatic responses— even those of love—could be diminished by familiarity. The novelty of silence awakened what habit had dimmed.

This was the first gift.

As I stepped into the shower, the upstairs phone rang and I jumped reflexively. And then, immediately, I remembered I was not talking and had no obligation to answer it. My shoulders dropped and my body released a tension I had not even been aware of holding. Only minutes from sleep and already my muscles had been primed to meet the day's demands. I thought of the sign at a local breakfast spot that reads:

Good morning. Let the stress begin.

I realized that we live our days with ears turned outward, ready to respond, always on the alert, almost as if we walked around holding huge ear trumpets to our heads, like figures in an old cartoon. But for this one day both my ears would be turned inward. I had only to listen to myself. Within the shower walls, it felt as if my world had grown smaller and smaller until all that was left was me.

Downstairs, I found that Hillary had already left for the day. The house was enveloped in stillness. No television. No music. I put out kibble for my cat, Sushi, and then set about making my own breakfast. As I worked, I gradually became aware of sounds surfacing: the hum of the furnace, the refrigerator motor, a pickup passing by on the street, the *tock-tock, tock-tock* of a blue jay pecking seed at the window feeder—all the sweet and comforting undertones of daily life.

Over the years I had prepared meals in quiet rooms, in *accidental* silence, as I would later come to call it, but I was discovering that intentional silence brought a focus to everything. Ordinary acts—measuring oats and water, chopping walnuts, scooping out a handful of raisins, stirring oatmeal—were transformed into meditations simply by the *attention* stillness brought to the tasks. Later, scrubbing out the gummy saucepan, I found unexpected pleasure in this simple job. I was experiencing what Buddhists have always taught: Silence, along with the attention it fosters, is our anchor to the present, to the here and now.

In the studio, I turned on the computer and set to work.

I had barely begun when the phone rang, breaking my concentration. As I had earlier in the shower, I tensed in a conditioned response. Although I listened to the caller's taped message, I did not pick up the receiver. A small choice, not answering, but one that held significance. By shutting myself away from the world, I was more whole unto myself.

.　　.　　.

I wrote until noon and then broke for lunch. Again, as I heated some leftover pea soup in the quiet kitchen and went about my normal life, I was aware of the acute mindfulness that attends stillness. Like the sea ducks I had observed on the beach the day before, I floated on an ocean of quietude, occasionally disappearing into reflection. Everything, including my own thoughts, seemed to be moving at a slower pace, as if in silence the ordinary measurements of time had been suspended. Or made elastic. As if minutes held the quantum equivalent of more hemoglobin.

Reveling in the peace and pleasure of our quiet home, I felt a corresponding quietness inside. My body and spirit felt cloaked in calmness, and yet I was more keenly aware of everything around me. Paradoxically, by wrapping myself in a cocoon of stillness, I was in some way engaging more fully with life rather than withdrawing from it.

Back at the desk, my writing flowed effortlessly. As I thought about this, I wondered if the energy that was normally dissipated in speech was going instead into the work. I had never before really thought about the physical toll that ordinary conversation extracts. I hadn't considered how fragmented attention shatters focus. Now I was experiencing complete focus as if for the first time.

Usually I finish writing by mid-afternoon, but that day I stayed at the computer much longer than usual. Yet when I finally returned to the kitchen to prepare dinner, I did not feel physically spent or emotionally exhausted from the lengthy hours at my desk. Rather, I was efficient, deeply rested, and at peace.

I had withdrawn for a day and the planet hadn't stopped mid-rotation. Margaret's mother had not died. Hope and Chris hadn't called. Hillary hadn't asked for a divorce. All was well.

Is this what happens when, even in the face of resistance, we follow our heart's desires? And what is the cost if we don't?

Thus began the quieting of my world. It was as if I were quenching a thirst I had long been unaware of. I had barely stepped over the threshold into silence, and yet my spirit felt calm, my soul serene, my heart open. By nightfall I knew only this: One day was not enough.

"Did you manage to do it?" a friend asked the next morning. When I had told her of my plan to spend a day not talking, she had bet me I wouldn't last an hour.

"Yes," I said.

"How was it?"

"Peaceful."

"It didn't feel weird?"

"Not really. Mostly it felt restful, meditative." Trying to explain, I suddenly thought of Anne Morrow Lindbergh. Although it had been at least a dozen years since I had read *Gift from the Sea*, I recalled Lindbergh's reflections on her need to be alone and how suspect that desire could be, and I remembered how deeply the words had resonated when I first read them.

"I don't know," my friend said. "An entire day without speaking. That's pretty radical."

Radical.

Oddly enough, another acquaintance had used that precise word when Hillary had described my foray into silence, as if the private and quiet act of choosing not to speak was the most astounding thing one could do, on par with running naked down Main Street, Chatham, or sabotaging a nuclear power plant. This coincidence sent me to the dictionary. I read that "radical" comes from the Latin *radicallis*: "of or going to the root of origin." So a radical digs to the root of things, goes deep.

Going deep, I knew, often leads to change. Was silence, then, to be a stone that would fall deep, reconfiguring the depths of my being, even as it sent ripples circling out? I released the thought almost as soon as it came, as I was not ready to consider its implications. I knew only that after this one day I felt profoundly rested and replenished, as if I had gone on a weekend retreat.

If this was the result of a single day of not speaking, I wanted more.

I wanted to return to this space of stillness, to further explore the grounds. When I had left the silent garden the night before, closing the gate behind me, I knew absolutely that I would return. And that it would be waiting for me.

CHAPTER 2

Snow Day

Walking INTO THE *Solitary Self*

AFTER HER DISCOVERY of the winter-cloaked garden, Mary Lennox was eager to go back. I, too, couldn't wait to experience again the magic of my special place.

·   ·   ·

When I was a child, I loved snow days and I still do. Each one seems a gift, a day with no "push" to it, a vessel for holding the season's treasures of peace, receptivity, and quiet. Remember waking the morning after it has snowed in the night? The atmospheric shift. Everything muted and new. Sharp edges softened. The contours of the land coated with white. Light refracted to silver. The day filled with mysterious promise.

Although it hadn't stormed, waking to silence on the second day was like that. By seeking stillness, I felt as if I were walking in fresh snow, leaving a single trail of footprints. My father, a farmer, used to tell me that a spring snow was nature's fertilizer because it brought nitrogen to the earth. As I lay in bed contemplating the snowlike quality of the day, I recalled this memory and smiled at the idea of silence as the fertilizer for the soil of my soul.

Snow Day

. .

Hillary was already up and out, off to fish the early-morning tide. I stretched, easing into the slowness of the day and relishing the quiet of our room. In truth, I was glad to be alone. Freed from any need to rush. Or to feel guilty about taking another day to myself.

The night before I had announced my intention to be silent again.

"How long are you going to do this?" Hillary had asked.

I shrugged. "I don't know. I've been thinking of doing it every other Monday."

"Every other Monday?" His voice revealed surprise and a note of displeasure.

"Yes." Then, trying to find a middle ground without rocking our marital craft, I asked, "Do you have a problem with that?"

"Well, it's inconvenient," he said.

"I know."

"And it's frustrating when I need to ask you something and you can't answer."

"I know," I said again.

"And what if someone calls you? What am I supposed to say?"

I felt a bolt of impatience—*Why couldn't he get it?*—but I made my voice reasonable. "Just tell them the truth," I said. "Tell them I'm having a day of silence."

I stayed for a while longer nestled in bed, falling back into stillness and listening. Again, as on the first day, it seemed as if things had slowed down, that time was irrelevant, artificial. Yet even as I experienced it, I found it difficult to fully accept the idea that this one change—the deliberate choice to forgo speech—could engender such a sense of peace. As I stared up through the skylight, it occurred to me that it might be my *intention* to keep silence in concert with my actual absence of speech that was reinforcing the sense of refuge. In other words, the experience was intensified because my silence was by commitment, not by accidental circumstance.

Finally, I rose and began making tracks through the white field of stillness.

With no phone to answer and no other interruptions, I was freed of that modern-day horror—multitasking. I thought about how fractured our attention often is. How, instead of being fully attentive to a phone conversation, often I would check e-mail, stir a pot on the stove, wander the house to complete chores that required only one hand, even play computer games. I remembered times in my life when this had not been true, times when the task of deadheading peonies or cleaning the basement or bathing a child had occupied me fully. I remembered the pleasure such focused attention brought to the most tedious chores. I recalled how even weeding the perennial beds became not a dreaded job to be gotten through, but a meditation with its own reward. I once read the honor of a job is in its execution. In silence, letting go of trying to do two or three things at once, I was rediscovering how attention can bring honor to the task at hand.

In the studio, again my writing flowed. Slowed down, my thoughts were more focused, and a pivotal scene in my novel, one I had struggled with for days, was suddenly resolved. Creativity and imagination require space to flower, and I had long known the truth of Picasso's statement, "Without great solitude no serious work is possible." Even so, once more I was surprised that something as simple as not speaking could produce such profound results. I was just beginning to consciously explore the connection between the space silence provides and its place in creating.

After lunch, I walked to the beach. I slowed my pace and gazed at the gray blue of the sky, listened to the wind singing in the grasses and the sound of my own breath, smelled the musty, organic odor of the marsh at low ebb. I was more attentive than usual, my senses sharper. Perceptions, dulled by familiarity, reawakened. Seeking stillness, I was rediscovering sounds.

One summer when I was teaching a creative writing workshop in Kenmare, Ireland, I learned an Irish phrase, *tuning the five-string harp*, which means opening the five senses and bringing them into alignment so they work in consonance. I love this image and the ancillary awareness that to become fully alive to life around us we must sensitize ourselves. The tuning of any instrument—viola, harp, or body—requires patience. It can't be forced or hurried. I was reminded of this phrase as I walked along the shore because it seemed that silence was serving as a tuning fork, awakening the five-string harp of my senses. It roused me to vibrations in the air around me, to whispers below the radar of ordinary life. Silence opened, sensitized, and softened me. It slowed me down and in doing so brought me into accord with my world, into harmony with myself and with nature.

Again and again in the coming years, I would come to this realization. And each time I would wonder how it is that we drift so far away from this rich and quiet place.

When I was young, a friend showed me how to hold an empty conch shell to my ear in order to hear the ocean's echo. Now, on the beach, I picked one up from the sand. Like all conchs found in the north, it was coarser in contour than its tropical cousin, the interior tinted orange rather than pink. I raised it to my ear. *Listen,* it seemed to say. *Listen to what sounds are hidden in the most unexpected places. Listen to what you can hear when you're not speaking.* It seemed a totem of silence, and I carried it home to place on my desk.

In the late afternoon, my day's work completed, I entered our library and scanned the bookshelves for my copy of Anne Morrow Lindbergh's *Gift from the Sea.* I have always felt an affinity for Lindbergh for the simple and rather silly reason that we share the same given name, both spelled with an *e* on the end. This sense of connection deepened when, like the author, I became a private pilot. For years, I collected her writings; *Gift from the Sea* was my favorite. The first time I read it I was a young mother and her reflections about a woman's need to seek and find solitude resonated deeply, although, at the time, there had seemed little possibility for it in my own life. Since my first day of silence, feeling a reawakened tie to Lindbergh, I had intended to read it again to see if my memory held true or if I had misremembered her philosophies and overlaid them with my own needs.

There it was on a bottom shelf, its blue dust jacket faded

and its spine worn. I brewed a pot of green tea, and then—porcelain mug beside me—settled in to read. Minutes passed. In the next room, the phone rang. I heard Hillary answer.

"Oh, hi, Betsy," he said, then, "No. She's not here right now. I'm not sure when she'll be back. Can I give her a message?"

She's not here right now. I looked with amazement at the passage open on my lap: "But if one says: I cannot come because it is my hour to be alone, one is considered rude, egotistical or strange. What a commentary on our civilization, when being alone is considered suspect; when one has to apologize for it, make excuses, hide the fact that one practices it—like a secret vice."

I flipped to the front of the book and looked for the publication date. Lindbergh had written these words in 1955.

The soul, Jung said, is inexorably driven to seek balance.

Today, for most of us, life is seriously out of balance, even more so than when Lindbergh's book was published. We have become inundated with obligations and, if you are at all like me, overwhelmed by noise and the onslaught of news and information, surrounded by clamor and meaningless conversations, all buttressed by our culture's supposition that action is preferable to inaction, busywork to idleness. Too many of us have bought into the idea that the pursuit of happiness is in fact the pursuit of pleasure. Somehow we have become estranged from quiet and have developed not only a low tolerance for it, but an almost outright fear of it.

Not too long ago, periods of reflection and stillness were woven into the fabric of our days as we washed dishes, prepared meals, chopped wood, mended clothing, and walked in contemplative silence. Technology has not only accelerated the pace of our lives, it has made our lives noisier and destroyed their peaceful rhythms.

Noise is a form of violence done to us, but we have become so accustomed to it that it barely registers, like a car alarm that blares on and on but which no one heeds. Sound systems have become part of our communal landscape, inescapable in supermarkets, shopping malls, ballparks, elevators, coffee shops and restaurants, office waiting rooms and hospitals. It's as if we have come to believe that silence is a void that must be filled whatever the cost. We no longer know how to be still. We no longer know how to be alone. We seem to require constant and relentless input. We are addicted to sensory overstimulation.

As we'll see later, this addiction comes at a tremendous

cost, physically, psychologically, and spiritually. It leaves us depleted, exhausted, and depressed. It negatively impacts our health, distances us from intimacy, and severs our connections with our internal selves. According to the U.S. Census Bureau, noise is now the number-one neighborhood complaint. Not crime. Noise.

As I write this chapter, I am in a small midwestern town on the edge of a tall-grass prairie working at the Ragdale Foundation, a retreat dedicated to creating a quiet refuge for artists. Yet even here, in this place whose sole purpose is to establish a center of peace, the noise of technology invades. For the last hour I have heard the steady and intrusive howl of a leaf blower outside my window, far, far removed from the comforting, cadenced scrape of tines against earth as my father raked sugar maple leaves in the yard of my childhood home. I'm aware, too, of the insistent hum of my computer and the lower-pitched one of my printer. Outside my door, a staff member vacuums the carpet on the stairs. From a distance I hear the train heading for Chicago. A jet screams overhead. Closer, in a nearby studio, someone is talking on a cell phone, although this is frowned upon. Over lunch, another writer, returning from swimming laps at the college natatorium, tells me rock music is now piped into the pool.

Snow Day

"Nothing has changed the nature of man so much as the loss of silence," the Swiss philosopher Max Picard wrote in 1948. "The invention of printing, technics, compulsory education—nothing has so altered man as this lack of relationship to silence, this fact that silence is no longer taken for granted, as something natural as the sky above or the air we breathe. Man who has lost silence has not merely lost one human quality but his whole structure has been changed thereby."

Nothing has changed the nature of man so much as the loss of silence.

Oceanographic studies have shown that boat traffic has elevated the noise level in the ocean to such a degree it is drowning out the sounds whales make to communicate. Like whales, we, too, suffer loss of communication because of noise. At wedding receptions, DJs crank up the volume to such a level that guests can't converse. Restaurants have become so noisy with blaring background music that dinner conversation is nearly impossible. At multiplexes, the soundtrack of one movie blasts so loudly it infiltrates the adjacent theater and competes with that of the film on the screen. It is exhausting just thinking of it.

According to studies, this unrelenting noise leads to hypertension, hearing loss, stress, and anxiety. To alleviate this tension and to numb discontent, we seek diversion, often by searching for more. More food. More drink. More things to do. More products to consume compulsively. More noise. We turn to iPods, televisions, and cellular phones— false companions that seem to assuage insecurity, loneliness, and anxiety, but in truth only add to them, like drinking a double espresso to calm frenzied nerves. Meanwhile, the number of antidepressants and sleeping pills being prescribed rises, and even young children are being diagnosed and treated for depression.

As Lindbergh wrote more than fifty years ago, "Not knowing how to feed the spirit, we try to muffle its demands in distractions. Instead of stilling the center, the axis of the wheel, we add more centrifugal activities to our lives— which tend to throw us off balance."

But our spirit has an instinct for silence. Every soul innately yearns for stillness, for a space, a garden where we can till, sow, reap, and rest, and by doing so come to a deeper sense of self and our place in the universe. Silence is not an absence but a presence. Not an emptiness but repletion. A filling up.

We require aloneness to develop mind and soul. For millennia spiritual seekers, religious teachers, and philosophers have recognized the value of solitude and contemplation and have made them an integral part of their lives. Buddhism, Christianity, Shamanism, Judaism, Hinduism, Sufism, Taoism, and Islam all have at their foundations a history of seeking solitude and silence as a path to the Source.

"Silence," Confucius said, "is the friend who never betrays."

Melville wrote that it is "the one and only voice of God."

Jesus went into the desert. Muhammad went to the cave of Mount Hira. Buddha sat beneath the Boddhi tree. Young Mary Lennox found the secluded garden.

And I went to a January beach.

.　.　.

"Too many words," a woman said to me in a dream several weeks before that first day of silence. When I woke, I laughed at the irony. As a journalist and novelist, I earn my living with words. I have always been gregarious and am an avid reader. Our home has three televisions, five radios, a CD and tape player, four two-line telephones, two cell phones, two computers, and one answering machine. I have not yet given in to the Apple advertising machine and purchased an iPod, but my car has a radio, tape deck, and CD player. Like so many of us, I am primed for speech, wired for sound.

Was it my soul then, as Jung suggested, that drove me to seek balance through silence?

Was this what had drawn me to the shore that January day? Or perhaps, without my being conscious of it, it had been the need to feel connected to something bigger than myself, as well as to connect with the deepest part of myself.

I was a seeker without a name for what I was seeking.

The morning after that second silence day, Hillary reminded me to return Betsy's call.

"I'm just curious," I said, careful to keep my voice even since this was still an unresolved subject between us. "I overheard you tell her I'd gone out. Why didn't you tell her what I asked you to say—that I was having a day of silence?"

"I don't know," he said. "It seemed too hard to explain. It was easier to say you weren't here."

"You really don't like me doing this, do you?" I said.

He hesitated, torn between the love and support he usually offered and his resistance to and discomfort with these quiet days. "It's kind of a pain in the ass," he finally said.

"I know," I said, eager to smooth things over. "I know it's frustrating and inconvenient."

"That sounds like you're going to do it again," he said. "Are you?"

I nodded. Again, I had closed the gate behind me when I walked away from my garden of quiet to return to my normal speaking life, and again I knew it would be waiting for me. Earlier I had marked off the second Monday of that month's calendar page with one word: *Silence*.

In truth, I was a bit smug about my "practice." Two days of stillness and I was a convert, a devoted oblate. Oh, yes, I was the guru of silence.

But when the Monday arrived, doubts began to surface.

CHAPTER 3

Compost

Confronting the Messy Space Within

WHEN SHE FIRST gained entry to the secret garden, Mary Lennox felt a rush of delight at her discovery of this hidden place. But soon, as she began to explore, she encountered brambles and tangled thickets. Around her were dead rose canes, matted leaves, and the other inevitable consequences of neglect and abandonment.

On the third Monday of silence, I woke, nerves jangled, with no trace of anticipation. That earth-blanketed-in-snow softness of the previous experience was as remote as Neptune. Instead I was possessed by a low-grade, free-floating anxiety I couldn't identify, and the very last thing I wanted to do was stay quiet, although the night before I'd had no forewarning, no sense of disquiet, only anticipation. The gate was open, the quiet space waited, but I was filled with resistance, reluctant to cross the threshold into the garden.

I did a quick mental scan for worries—Hillary, my work, friends, money, Hope and Chris, who were both away at college—but could name no source of my disquiet, just the jittery sense that something was off-kilter. I felt as if I'd mainlined a triple shot of caffeine. Downstairs, in the kitchen, I flicked on the television. (From the first, I had set out with one simple goal—to refrain from speech—and on that day I had not yet formulated rules about what outside noise I would let in or whether I would answer e-mail, watch news or movies, or listen to music. I chose instead to allow the specific structure of these days to unfold gradually.)

The morning news revealed details of war crimes in Serbia, the mounting death toll from a gas explosion in a Turkish coal mine, and a report from a committee on bioethics that was investigating members of Congress. These thorny dispatches did nothing to calm me, but served only to intensify my anxiety. I switched off the TV and set about scrambling some eggs.

After breakfast, still edgy and craving distraction, I wandered from room to room trying to settle down. Amazingly, in the midst of my jumbled thoughts, I recalled the words of St. Benedict: "The ease with which aimless desire can disturb our hearts." They seemed so truthful, but what did I desire?

Well, for starters, to escape.

The house felt too empty, too quiet. I would rather have eaten a beach blanket than take on the burden of another day of silence. I wanted to call a friend and make plans for lunch or shopping. But when I reached for the phone, I hesitated. If I broke my commitment to silence, would I ever return to it? Or would the key be lost, the gate forever locked? I turned away and headed for the studio at the end of the hall. But once there I didn't even switch on my computer. Let's face it. This day, my garden was a mess.

I was irritable. Lonely. Rudderless. Bored with a capital, bold, underscored *B*. I might have ceased verbal speech, but my monkey mind was chattering at full speed: *Staying silent is pointless. Why am I doing this anyway?*

What do you do when you are struck with a free-floating anxiety? When you're stuck in the can't-hit-a-moving-target mode?

I bargained with myself: I would keep quiet until noon. A half day of silence was better than nothing. I could surely handle three more hours, and then I would call a friend and seek some shop therapy. With this plan, the tension eased so that I was able to settle at my desk.

Before I began, I took a deep breath, allowed my shoulders to drop, and gradually immersed myself in work. The next time I glanced at the clock I was amazed to find that it was after twelve. The morning's bargain had centered me so that I knew I could stay in silence for the remainder of the day. My heart was calmer, some of the turmoil eased, and the need for distraction and escape no longer felt urgent.

But underneath, something continued to brew. The restlessness—though muted—was still there.

Outside, the weather had turned raw—a bleak February day with slate skies and a wind that bit. I bundled up with parka and scarf and started out for a walk. And suddenly, as I headed toward the shore and my own narrow swath on the sound, my body was weighted with a sorrow that felt marrow-deep and ancient.

Certainly there was plenty in the world to grieve about. Perhaps this heart heaviness had been triggered by the brief exposure to the morning news: the hundreds who had died in the coal mine; man's inhumanity and capacity for cruelty playing out in Serbia; the confusion and chaos of the world.

But as I continued walking, seeds of other, more personal disappointments and disconnections took root. Silence may hollow the empty space essential for something to enter, but what appears is not always lovely. I found myself thinking about sad and hurtful things. I thought about my mother and how we both avoided honest conversations that might touch on painful subjects (family dysfunction and estrangement, alcohol abuse, my sister's death), and how this defined so much of my relationship with her.

"At least we aren't like those Italian families," she would

tell me when I was growing up. "I never have been able to understand how families can shout all kinds of terrible things at each other. Things that can never be forgiven or forgotten."

No, we weren't like that. In our house, words of anger were sealed inside. My sisters and I were forbidden to slam doors or raise our voices to our parents. Even falling silent in their presence was not safe. We were accused of sulking, of being moody, and told to smile. Another kind of silence entirely.

Once, while writing a contribution for an anthology about what daughters had always wanted to tell their mothers, I told her the essay was the most difficult thing I had ever written.

"Why?" she asked.

I reached across the table and took her hand. "You taught me to be silent," I answered.

"And that's what my parents taught me," she responded.

I reflected on all my unresolved issues with my mother, ones I believed long ago put to rest, and I swallowed tears.

Now I understood. This was what I had wanted to run from.

"The quieter we become," said Ram Dass, "the more we hear."

And perhaps that is exactly why we avoid becoming silent, why we fill the air with meaningless chatter and music and talk radio and all manner of chewing gum for the mind. On some level, perhaps—being quiet—we are afraid of what we will hear.

As the Indian philosopher and teacher J. Krishnamurti said, "You try being alone, without any form of distraction, and see how quickly you want to get away from yourself and forget what you are."

"We can sweep things under the carpet until we have amassed a mountainous heap," a therapist once told me, "and we can crawl over it and pretend that it's not there, but inevitably the time will come when we'll fracture a leg climbing over that pile while crossing the room."

On that February day, as it has many times since, intentional silence was serving as a yellow light in my path, halting my stride, leading me to recognize matters shoveled beneath the rug. And forcing me to acknowledge that I was out of right relationship with my world.

Like many people, perhaps like you, I don't want to think of myself as a woman who harbors resentment, let alone anger, but stillness had brought me face-to-face with my own complexities and contradictions. My hidden aches and anguish.

Well.

All was fine and dandy when silence sparked creativity and restored me, when it slowed me down and made me more attentive to the world around me, but now that it had made me more aware of the world within, I felt ambushed, my feet tripped by the underbrush and brambles of neglected space. Small wonder we avoid solitude and stillness, I thought, as the unresolved family issues tightened my heart. Small wonder we fill our days with activity and every form and fashion of noise or that everywhere in our culture addictions provide means for disengaging from ourselves. Like the U2 song about running so hard to stand still. Who in her right mind wants to sit quietly and pay attention to what dwells within? Who wants to confront unhappiness? Or family disconnects? Who wants to face mortality?

Who wants to deal with any of that?

.   .   .

In Stanley Kunitz's poem "The Round" he writes about sitting at his desk in his basement studio in Provincetown, Massachusetts, and gazing out at the bloated heap of compost outside his window, the "steamy old stinkpile" where things decompose and break down. Within each of us there resides our own muddy, messy space, our inner garbage heap where we toss scraps too painful to consider or confront, the loss, pain, grief, and disappointment that are all too real. In the hollow of our hearts reside the fault lines of our lives, the lies we tell ourselves to get by, and the space where narcissistic aspects of personality can arise. When we weed out extraneous stimulation and let go of the reins of control, these things claim our attention. As a minister friend once told me, "In silence, all the deformed children that dwell inside come forward and say 'Love me.'" And this is what we flee. Kathleen Norris writes of this in *The Cloister Walk* when she notes, "Any life lived attentively is disillusioning as it forces us to know us as we are."

And it is silence that allows us the space and stillness in which to think about our motives, to examine our behavior, to see where we've fallen short. It is only when we drag our smallest, shabbiest parts into the light that we can move toward becoming whole.

Of course, it is the thought of confronting those shabby, prickly, shame-based selves that makes us want to run, to avoid being still, to fill our lives with activity and noise. With companions real and virtual.

In his book *Sabbath*, Wayne Muller tells of a Native American woman who leads people into the wilderness on vision quests, three days spent alone during which each participant listens for teachings that come when one takes a sacred journey. She told Muller that most people are not as afraid of the dangers that lurk in the darkness and wilderness as they are anxious about having to confront what will surface from within when they are faced with solitude and stillness. The alluvial sludge. The abyss.

Compost.

Muller's story reminds me of a *Calvin and Hobbes* strip in which the cartoonist Bill Watterson drew the boy and his tiger walking outside, and Hobbes says, "When you're confronted with the stillness of nature, you can even hear yourself think." Calvin responds, "This is making me nervous. Let's go in."

So, of course, like Calvin confronting stillness or those setting out on vision quests, we often want to run away. To escape the restlessness of our souls. To jack up the world's noise until it is loud enough to drown out the clamor and bury the stink emanating from our personal compost piles, noises that have one name: fear.

And this is the largest fear of all: Once quiet, we will hear an inner voice proclaim, "You are not enough."

So why not just avoid the compost? Why not skirt the stinking heap?

For centuries poets and philosophers, theologians and

therapists have taught us that turning over these compost piles is a risk we must undertake, for within these same mounds lies the fertile matter out of which new life arises and is nourished, a cyclic alchemy always at play, just as it is in any garden. This is the necessary work, the means of discovering spirit and self, a call that must be heeded. We do this by going deep. That is our charge. As the fourteenth-century Sufi poet Hafiz wrote:

> *Don't surrender your loneliness*
> *So quickly.*
> *Let it cut more deep.*

So there I was again in the fantasy of wanting life to be neat. Of wanting myself to be "evolved" and beyond petty personal concerns. I wanted, as well, to be in right relationship with myself and those in my world. Instead I was sitting smack dab in the middle of the messiness of existence, confronting hard work I would prefer to avoid.

I would rather have had a root canal *redone* than face the truth of old familial wounds. That night, as I reflected on the day, I understood that if I was to attain any measure of inner peace, I would have to till the soil of my heart.

I had not resolved the issue with my mother that day, but

the surrounds of stillness had brought me some measure of clarity, like silt-thick water that clears when it is allowed to stand still. I had come to understand that we begin to release discomfort and pain only by first really experiencing them. As Jung stated, "There is no coming to life without pain." Silence was serving as the portal through which I was beginning to come fully to life. It was the key and the gate, as well as the garden itself.

I had only begun to root around in my garden and to discover the work ahead. I was just beginning to understand that, within the surrounds of solitude, necessary questions would come to light that would lead ultimately to self-discovery.

Who am I?

What is my calling? And how do I cultivate it?

How do I get home?

That third Monday my commitment began. Silence was no longer a whim but, I realized, essential for my soul. I saw that there was something to be learned in the everyday—in all the joys and sorrows and pains and tasks as ordinary as scrubbing a dirty floor. But mostly our busy worlds are too noisy for us to pay attention. We don't touch the rawness of the truth until we stop.

Compost

I didn't know where silence would direct me in the future, only sensed that it was part of a journey to a deeper connection with others that would help put the "me" back in myself.

I went to my studio and turned on the computer. I selected a straightforward font and typed these words: "I Am Having a Day of Silence." I printed the sentence out and pasted it on a three-by-five-inch index card, which I then covered with wide strips of clear tape to strengthen and protect it. The fashioning of the card was a small act. It took, at most, no more than ten minutes. And yet it felt significant, a firming of a pledge I had made with myself and a sign that I was ready to reveal my practice to the world beyond my immediate circle of family and friends.

In a universe filled with tumult, stress, and the siren calls of distractions, I knew that, more than ever, coming to this garden—spading over compost, weeding and planting, even sitting in the sun—was necessary work.

CHAPTER 4

Beach Stones

Creating Necessary Boundaries

THE FACT THAT it was bound by brick walls was, from the first, one of the most intriguing aspects of the secret garden for young Mary. She "liked still more the feeling that when its beautiful old walls shut her in no one knew where she was."

I, too, liked the way a proclaimed day of silence enclosed me in a private space. At times it felt as if I were encapsulated in an invisible bubble or a protective cloud, in the world but not of it. On those Mondays, I had no obligation to respond to the people who populated my universe. Like all gardeners, I was learning that plots are more easily maintained when set apart in some way, whether by hedges, paths, or walls.

But a fence—whether formed by brick or silence—excludes others even as it shuts us in. And so, of course, that meant that occasionally the people in my life felt shut out, rejected, or simply irritated by the boundary that I insisted on maintaining. And their discomfort gave rise to my own.

As I walked to the beach on this particular March day, gusts blew in from the northeast, foretelling a storm to come, and a full-moon tide flooded the marsh. The grasses—shades of straw and mocha—were broken or bent nearly horizontal by winter and wind. A half dozen mallards and a blue heron, seeking the lee, had gathered at a curve in the saltwater creek that traversed the flats.

A verse I used to read to my children long ago played in my mind:

> *The March wind doth blow and we shall have snow.*
> *And what will poor robin do then?*
> *He'll fly to the barn to keep himself warm*
> *And hide his head under his wing. Poor thing.*

Like the robin in the nursery rhyme and the birds in the marsh, I, too, sought escape. Not from the winds. From the storm brewing back at my house.

My friend Heather, a tall, elegant, redheaded Brit, is a landscaper and organic gardener. During that winter, with her regular work slow, she occasionally helped out with the upkeep of our home. Earlier that morning, when she'd arrived, I'd shown her my "I Am Having a Day of Silence" card. She read it but said nothing. We exchanged hugs and then, with all prospects of small talk eliminated, I'd walked down the hall to my study. That went well, I'd thought. It hadn't proved too awkward.

But soon my concentration was broken. Pots banged, cupboard doors slammed. Even the vacuum seemed especially loud, making it impossible to concentrate. I closed the French doors that separate my studio from the rest of the house, but still the racket prevailed. Heather swore, vivid curses mitigated only slightly by her British lilt.

I tried to convince myself that whatever was going on had nothing to do with me. She'd probably had an argument with her boyfriend. *It is not my problem.* Still, I was anxious.

I was used to smoothing things over. Now, in silence, I was impotent and powerless. Had it been a "speaking day" I would already be in the kitchen, boiling tea water and inviting Heather to the table to talk. Now she was clearly upset and I couldn't ask why. Something was wrong and I couldn't fix it. Basically, I wanted her anger to evaporate. It was so *huge* and intimidating, like a nor'easter that sweeps in with driving rain, dissolving furrows, exposing seeds. Minutes passed. The din didn't cease. I wrestled my urge to go to her, to find out what was wrong, to break silence. Finally, needing to do *something*, I grabbed my parka and headed out.

Now, at the beach, I sat on a weathered wooden bench and stared out at the whitecaps. Even with the parka hood tied tightly around my head, I heard the roaring wind and crashing surf. A man approached, his head and torso bent into the weather. I turned my face away to avoid the potential awkwardness of not responding should he say hello.

Though I grew chilled, I stayed on. I was tense and anxious at the prospect of returning to the house, where, in silence, I could do nothing but bear witness to Heather's anger.

Do you also find it difficult to sit and listen to another's anger? Do you, too, want to avoid another's pain, whether in the form of grief, rage, or disappointment? Are you like me in that you find it awkward to simply stand as a witness and not fix the problem?

When I speak of my silent days, women often say, "I could never do that." I understand. Most of us are "fixers." One aspect of withdrawing from speech is that we have to cede influence over others. To be speechless is to relinquish control, to know that there is nothing we can do, including expressing empathy in the face of another's distress. At heart, silence is an exercise in surrender.

A Buddhist friend told me that she deals with anger and fear, both hers and that of others, by welcoming them.

"What do you mean?" I asked.

"Whenever I'm having fear I say, 'Oh, fear, my old friend. Have a seat.'"

Have a seat. Old friend.

Right.

Must we really welcome fear into our lives like a fond companion? And what about anger or other emotions that bring discomfort? How do we welcome them?

As I sat at the beach I realized that I was a long way from Zen. Finally I rose to leave. A small gray rock, one of many spilled along the wrack line, caught my eye, and I stooped to pick it up. It was wet and gritty in my palm. A narrow band of white was penciled down the middle, perfectly bisecting the gray. *Boundaries,* it seemed to say. Fences.

Of course sitting in silence not only meant surrendering the reins of control. It was also an opportunity to explore boundaries. To think about where I ended and another began. To cede jurisdiction over another's mood, no matter how uncomfortable it felt.

I clutched the bisected stone in my hand and headed back, determined to accept Heather's right to her anger even as I recognized that I wasn't completely at ease with it, even in some way felt responsible for it.

At home, I was greeted by quiet. I set the stone on the sill above the kitchen sink.

"Hi," Heather said.

I turned.

She was smiling, as if the earlier nor'easter had never occurred.

"I just have to tell you," she said as she pulled on her coat. "This morning your silence really made me angry."

I picked up the gray rock again, cupped its sea-smoothed surface.

"It was hard to stay here with you not talking," she said.

I fingered the narrow white stripe.

"At first it just made me uncomfortable," she continued, "but then I began getting mad and I couldn't figure out why. I guess I thought that because you weren't talking, you were angry with me."

I smiled, trying to convey that I was not upset in any way.

"But after a while," she said, "I realized what I was really mad about." She paused and drew a breath. "My mother used silence as a weapon. Her silence was so punishing it could slice you like a knife."

I set the rock on the sill and turned back to Heather. Our eyes met. I understood. As a child, I, too, had known that kind of icy silence.

In my childhood home my parents did not yell. Their anger was disguised in thin-lipped, cold-eyed, punitive silence, one that fostered guilt and left you guessing what you'd done wrong. It was a silence far more threatening and isolating than whatever words might have been spoken. But emotion subverted does not go away. Rather, it is transmuted.

My sister Sandy committed suicide when she was thirty-six. For years I was haunted by a specific memory. She stood in the kitchen, furious, and swung the door open, ready to slam it. One look from my father and she shut it quietly.

Suicide is complicated and seldom does one event hold the clue. Certainly my sister's life was full of loss and disappointments. She eloped at sixteen and became a mother at seventeen. When she was nineteen her son was killed in an accident. She was divorced when she was in her thirties. Today, when I think of her death, I picture that day in the kitchen, the door swung wide in the silent room. I remember how it felt to wait and watch, both hoping and fearing she would find the courage to slam it shut.

In our family today, her death is still cloaked in silence, as was much of her life.

"Silence in families," my friend Ginny said. "You could write an entire book about it."

"Tell me," I said, rolling my eyes.

Before she left that day, Heather shared one more thought.

"After a while," she said, "I realized how different your silence was from my mother's. You showed me silence could be neutral. Even gentle."

In "speaking mode," I would have said this to Heather: Not all silence is punishing. Not all silence is meant to disempower. But words had not been needed. Silence had spoken for me.

So again a silent day surprised me. I had begun by anticipating the quiet only to encounter anger. And then came the challenge of surrendering control in the face of Heather's mood. I have never been adept at establishing boundaries, but silence had created one for me. In its tender way, and in spite of my discomfort, it was tutoring me in the importance of appropriate bounds.

I once read that the Inuit and Igloolik have more than two hundred words for snow, and I envy them a language that can encompass the many subtleties of a single idea. I've read, too, that in the Buddhist tradition of Southeast Asia there are twenty-one different words for silence. In my dictionary, few synonyms are listed. *Muteness. Stillness.* A thesaurus doesn't offer many more. *Quiescence. Peace. Wordlessness. Quietude. Quiet.*

But just as there are countless varieties of lilies, there are different kinds of silence, as many as there are intentions and reasons behind it. It can be gentle and peaceful. Risky and brave. Angry and punishing. Thoughtful and wise. Intimate. Loving. Restorative. Reflective. Sacred or profane. It can be used to honor or to shame. To diminish or empower.

How many words would it require to reveal all its multitudinous nuances and intents?

Fifty?

Two hundred?

More?

PART TWO

Cultivation

CHAPTER 5

Bittersweet Vine

Pruning Invasive Species

MARY ENTERED THE GARDEN IN WINTER and so could not tell what was alive and what was not. But as she explored, she saw green points pushing their way up through the matted brown grass.

"She searched about until she found a rather sharp piece of wood and knelt down and dug and weeded out the weeds and grass until she made nice little clear places around them. 'Now they look as if they could breathe,' she said."

Long ago, in the fall, I used to cut branches of Oriental bittersweet and bring them into the house. When the vines had dried and the bright orange-red outer shell of the berries had cracked open to reveal the yellow kernel inside, I would weave the vines into wreaths for the front door or create centerpieces for our table. After the holidays, I'd toss the vines into the wooded lot next to our home. Gradually, over the years, the vines took hold and spread, encroaching on and choking our rhododendrons and forsythia. Years later, I learned that bittersweet is not native to Cape Cod. It had been introduced long ago and now, like many other nonindigenous plants, it was spreading rapidly and proving to be a nuisance.

It seems the perfect metaphor for our lives today. What is at first appealing can over time become invasive. The only way to reverse the situation is to start pruning.

Our realtor called this morning. She specializes in summer rental properties and was calling to see if we had yet arranged for Wi-Fi at our cottage. She said Internet access is expected by vacationers so they can keep in touch with their offices and continue to work. Apparently the days of lazy summer living in a simple cottage by the shore have vanished. Tenants today require not only washers and dryers, dishwashers, air conditioning, hot tubs, and gas grills, but cable television, answering machines, Wi-Fi, DVD players, and sophisticated sound systems as well.

"We are so connected today," another writer recently said to me. She was referring to cell phones and e-mail and BlackBerry.

But being reachable doesn't mean being connected. In fact, technology often leads to a greater disconnect. As the Swiss philosopher Max Picard noted in *The World of Silence*, it is technology that has both dramatically altered our lives and increased the speed at which we live to a point where our days are dictated and dominated by clocks and calendars. The introduced species—cell phones, pagers, text messages, computers, faxes, telephones, answering machines, voice mail, e-mails—have encroached on our time and made us instantly available. And because we can be accessible, it is expected of us.

Demands of all kinds weave like vines through our lives. We have come to accept pressing schedules as normal and rest as an aberration. Stressed, anxious, and depleted, we rush through errands, appointments, and social engagements. We manufacture counterfeit necessities. We wedge in hours at the gym and carve out minutes for household errands, carpool runs, and committee meetings. Thus we spend moments and hours and days, weeks and months and years of our precious lives overworked, overbooked, and overcommitted, cramming more into every fragmented day. In the process, our perceptions are dulled and we are deaf to much of life around us. As psychologists and sociologists have noted, we have become human *doings* and not human *beings*.

There is no downtime. Even hours spent pursuing relaxation are crammed with activities, filled with noise.

Research shows that Americans spend an average of 974 hours a year listening to radio, 1,555 hours watching television, 86 hours playing video games, and 195 hours using the Internet—a statistic I suspect is already outdated. Patricia McDonough, senior vice president at Nielsen Media Research, notes that in this country, "There are more TVs than people and there's a TV, in many houses, in every room." The latest trend in home remodeling is having a flat-screen TV in the bathroom.

At entertainment events, the level of noise is deafening. Literally. During air shows featuring the navy's Blue Angels, as if the shriek of jet engines and roaring afterburners weren't rousing enough, ear-splitting rock music is amped into the air. And at major-league ballparks, ramped-up rock songs blast out at every inning break. Sports announcers responsible for relating plays on the field are never silent. The chatter is endless. Do you find it as telling as I do that in broadcasting lingo, moments of silence on air are called "dead time" and are to be avoided like an eighth deadly sin? Talk radio would more aptly be named shout radio. Indeed, when Achak Deng, a Sudanese refugee, attended an NBA game in this country last year, he thought the loudness and lewdness of the pre-show festivities were "perfectly designed to drive people insane."

In a sermon he preached at the Knox Presbyterian Church in Cincinnati, Ohio, "Taking Time Out Before Time Runs Out," the Reverend Thomas D. York observed that "Americans generally suffer from the grand illusion that nothing important is happening unless it is accompanied by a great deal of loud noise."

And so we jack up noise and activity in an attempt to feel alive, just as film directors hype up the soundtrack in chase scenes in order to elevate a sense of excitement. We have come to equate peace and serenity with boredom. We have forgotten what is of real significance. We create lives of false urgency and overloaded schedules so that we feel important. We paddle harder and harder to navigate in a whirlpool of noise and demands that we ourselves have created.

. . .

Worse are the burdens we have laid on our children, passing on to them our ambitions and anxieties, robbing them of the free time necessary for daydreaming and discovery. Today's parents share stories of days packed with classes, lessons, after-school activities, and 4:00 a.m. drives to hockey rinks because that's the only ice time available for practice or games. It was not always so. In the past, sewn into the rhythm of a child's life were hours unstructured and rich, free from demands and obligations. Those are the times I remember most when I think of my childhood. Like Mary Lennox in her garden, I knew stretches of silence and solitude that brought me back to a sense of wonder and imagining and to the peaceful place necessary for developing character.

On winter afternoons, as soon as the school bus released me at the foot of our drive, I tore toward our house. And to freedom. Once inside, I dropped my books, traded my school clothes for play clothes, grabbed my skates, and then, with my collie, Lady, as my only companion, I crossed the road in front of our house and headed for an iced-over swamp. There, I sat on the frozen surface, stripped off my mittens and boots, pulled on my skates and laced them with fingers quickly growing clumsy and numb with cold. When I finished, I rose to glide along the length of the stream that traversed the center of the swamp. I wove in and around the clumps of dried grasses and reeds, skating on and on, as the December sky darkened toward late afternoon. This was a time long before Sony Walkmans or iPods and earbuds. As my breath formed clouds in the air, the only sound cutting through the silence was that of my blades stroking the ice, and, beneath that, the symphony of life around me on an ordinary winter afternoon. The occasional creaking of the ice beneath my skates. The hum of passing traffic on the distant road. The rustle of leaves as Lady investigated a clump of dried reeds.

Even at that young age, I already felt mounting pressures to succeed in school, but as I skated on and on, the daylight turning to dusk, I shed their weight. I played tag with my dog, laughing when she slid sideways on the ice. For a time, I raced the length of the frozen stream in long even strokes until I was breathless, and then I skated circles, forming patterns on the ice, not unlike silent whirlpools. Eventually, driven by thirst, I sat, and, using the rear point of my skate blade as a pick, I chipped away at the ice, chopping until I created a hole large enough for water to rise up. Then I flopped prone, legs splayed behind me, and drank.

This is what I remember: the shock in my chest when the frigid liquid hit; then, on my tongue, the wild taste of untamed water, fertile with unknown life and hidden dangers. This bog water was far removed from the purified, odorless stuff I was used to. It was alive. Yet as I drank, rather than feeling apprehension, I felt profoundly connected to the earth and to this particular spot where much later in the spring I would return armed with a Mason jar to scoop up pollywogs. Lying on the ice, I was strengthened and nurtured by the primeval taste of nature, just as, alone on the winter afternoon, I was being sustained and invigorated by silence and solitude.

As I grew up, I was weaned from wildness and had less free time to explore on my own. I became restrained, more fearful of wild things and more careful of what I was willing to take in. But I have never forgotten the jolt of the icy swamp water and how it satisfied something deeper than thirst, some nameless desire that is the urge to taste essential life. Was it this instinct that led me to silence?

      .   .   .

One Sunday night about a year after I had begun setting aside Mondays for silence, Hillary and I sat by the fire in the library. My book fell to my lap as I stared out at the snow falling soundlessly to the ground beyond the window, quieting the world. It was, I thought, a perfect precursor for the next morning, when I would again be silent.

Hillary broke into my musings. "You want anything?" he said. "Coffee? Tea?"

"Nothing," I said. "Thanks."

He got up to throw another log on the fire.

"Just so you remember," I said, "tomorrow's my silent day."

He took up the poker and shifted the logs, creating a meteor shower of sparks. I watched them flicker and die.

"You know," he said, "when you started this whole business, I didn't like it."

Not exactly a state secret. Nearly every first and third Monday he'd mutter how inconvenient my silence was. And even on the days when he didn't openly complain, he'd hit me with questions that couldn't be answered by a nod or shake of the head. *What time did Hope say she was coming home? Where did Chris say he was going today? What did you say you're doing tomorrow morning? When is my dentist appointment?*

I understood his frustration. It was not only my own life that was put on hold during the days I did not speak, it was *our* life. We were accustomed to the easy companionship of conversation; we relied on each other's availability. In addition to our individual work and a full social schedule, we shared a small business.

So although I had chosen silence, our whole family experienced the consequences. Discussions and decisions, both major and less significant ones, had to be put on hold. Social invitations for the first or third Mondays were precluded. Both our children spoke of the inconvenience of my nonavailability. Hope said she missed the possibilities for long walks or spontaneous lunches out, the occasion of much girl talk. Chris pointed out that dinners weren't as much fun when one person wasn't speaking. And like Hillary, both Hope and Chris found it frustrating when they needed to ask me something and I couldn't respond. My silence continually broke the settled rhythms of family life. And so some days I would feel selfish, and a cloak of guilt would settle on my shoulders. Other times, I'd feel indignant. What was the big deal? The only one it didn't seem to bother was Sushi. On my Mondays, she would curl up by my side or on the corner of my writing desk—a little sister-spirit in stillness.

.   .   .

Hillary turned back to the fire. "Not only don't I like it, but I get irritated when the rental agents call," he said and continued to poke at the logs. "Or our bank, or accountant. Or when we need to make a decision about something and you can't talk."

"So what are you saying?" I asked. "Are you asking me not to do it anymore?"

He turned toward me. "I just wanted to tell you," he said. "After a while, your silent days have taught me something I needed to learn."

"What's that?"

He smiled. "Most things just aren't that important."

Most things just aren't that important. But our culture does not support this idea. If anything, we are schooled to believe that everything is urgent. So how do we sort out our priorities? And what, amid the noise, makes us pause and explore the plot in which we live to distinguish what has become invasive? What is the tool you use to rake through the demands and intrusions of your life? For me, it was silence.

"There is more help and healing in silence than in all the useful things," Picard wrote. "It strengthens the untouchable, it lessens the damage inflicted by exploitation. It makes things whole again."

The problem is that silence does not fit easily into the world of profit and it is hard work to ignore the commercial values that dominate our society, what Thomas Merton called "the murderous din of our materialism." It is as if we are caught in an eddy of noise and constant activity, our legs pumping like pistons as we struggle to keep our heads above water. Until something stops us in our tracks.

A flat tire. A snowstorm. A power outage. An accident. Illness. Death.

Or silence.

Monday after Monday, in stillness, I was finding peace. It was affording me the opportunity to slow down, to step out of habitual behaviors. To sort priorities. To learn what mattered to me. Our society may undervalue silence because we cannot profit from it, but I was profiting by it. Each time, silence distanced me from fake demands and shook my life into perspective as I learned not to care so deeply about the insignificant. It gave me space to reflect and to discern what held value and what didn't.

I was learning the same lesson Hillary noted that evening by the fire: Most things just aren't that important. Moreover, not only were some things not important, many things were not even necessary.

In his sermon at Knox Presbyterian, Reverend York reminisced about the joys of rising early during a vacation by Lake Michigan. "To hear the world wake up before you can see it move is like being in the early stages of creation," he said. He then related how, for a few minutes, in the stillness of dawn, he'd watched a mother deer and her fawns emerge from the underbrush by the lake. "I couldn't help but ponder, what wonders we never see, what melodies we never hear traveling too fast to look or to listen."

How often do we race along at a speed too fast to attend to life around us? How frequently are we caught in the windstorm of noise and activity and thus unable to hear faint whispers that hold the power to stir our souls?

"The crust of the everyday must be broken through," wrote Eugène Delacroix.

Like the skate blade I used decades ago to break through pond ice in order to drink wild water, silence continues to break through barriers to touch what is real and connect me to the fecundity of life. It grabs me by the nape and shakes me, teaching me not to care so much or to hunger so often for the ephemeral and insignificant. It helps me discern the difference between flowering plants and weeds in the garden of my days.

There is a line in a poem by Mary Oliver that haunts with its question: "This one and glorious life you have. How will you spend it?"

How will we spend our lives? Spinning in the whirlpool of noise and activity? Or reflecting on a stone bench in the garden alcove?

With each passing Monday, I found myself wanting more and more to sit on the granite seat and bask in the sun. To identify and prune back invasive species. To weed and seed. And to discover what no longer was important.

And what was.

CHAPTER 6

Dragonfly

Discovering THE
Shadow Sides
OF *Silence*

AS THE MONTHS of silent Mondays passed, I found the din and clamor of modern life to grow more intolerable. And I had a growing appreciation of Thomas Merton's journal entry noting that noise made him love silence more and more. Like Merton, who sought even deeper solitude than that allowed within his Trappist monastery, and like Mary Lennox, who wanted to spend her entire day in the hidden garden, I was becoming more enamored with stillness and solitude.

I was coming to embrace silence, welcoming quiet Mondays for the gifts and teachings they brought and the time they allowed for reflection and restoration. I found myself wanting to share with others what I experienced. And then one evening, while in residence at an artists' colony, I was again reminded that not all silence was necessarily experienced as nurturing. Or even benign.

After dinner a group of us had gone to sit by the fire. While we sipped our wine, I gave an informal presentation on my silence practice. In my enthusiasm for silence and belief in its transformative powers, I no doubt sounded like a circuit rider preaching at the frontier. After I finished, Reza

Daneshvar, an Iranian-born writer who has been living in exile in Paris since 1982, approached me.

"You talk about silence with passion and love," he said.

I detected a note of reproach in his voice. "But. . . ," I said.

"But it is easy for you. You are a middle-class white woman in America with a nice family and home."

His words irritated me. I felt chastised and judged.

"For women in the East," he continued, "silence is not so nice. For them silence is a punishment. It is a means of suppression."

"I understand," I said, although I was growing angry. I felt that he was belittling my work and misunderstanding it.

"You must talk about this," he insisted. "How not all silence is benign."

I nodded but I was in no mood to listen. I decided he was drunk.

The next morning, Reza again approached me. "When I was in prison in Iran," he said, "silence was used as a form of torture."

His words chilled me. "As torture?"

Prisoners had been forbidden to speak, he said. There were times when he would welcome the approaching footsteps of his jailers just to hear sound, even though it usually meant he was going to be taken away to be beaten. "You must write about this, too," he said again.

Reza was right, of course. If I was to fully understand silence and my responses to it, as well as the reactions of those around me, I would have to dig deeper and explore its shadow sides as well.

As a child, I had known well this shadow side of silence. I feared *being* silenced.

In this memory, it is a morning in early August.

I am ten, a thin girl with brown braids and bruised shins, dressed in green hand-me-down shorts one size too large. I straddle a length of wooden fence, Lady at my feet. My sister Sandy sits to my left. She is two years older than I and alternately my tormentor and my protector. And I idolize her. She is the commander of our childhood ship and repository of the knowledge I use to navigate my world: how to tell when the pond ice is thick enough for skating, how to gauge my father's moods, how to listen to the radio under the covers at night without getting caught, and how to avoid a certain family friend whose hugs feel "funny."

Earlier, we begged our mother to take us swimming at the lake, but she has a migraine and has banished us from the house. Now, struck dumb with boredom and foot-dragging heat, we sit and stare at our father's cows. There are several brown Guernseys, valued for the high cream quality of their milk, and two Jerseys. The rest are high-producing Holsteins.

Sandy is trying to talk me into riding one of the Holsteins bareback, a trick we've tried before. I argue that it is too hot, too much work. First we'll have to get Lady to cut a cow off from the herd and corral her back to the barn, where we'll lock her in a stanchion and, ignoring her mooing protests and wild, rolling eyes, one of us will climb on her back and then the other will release her. Just the idea makes me sweat, as does the thought of the eventual consequences. Since the last time, our father has forbidden us to ride the cows, telling us it causes their milk to sour.

"We'll get in trouble," I say.

"You're such a chicken," she says.

"Am not," I automatically reply.

In fact, I am less daring than she and have a list of anxieties:

Heights.

Mice.

Snakes.

Getting lost in the cornfield.

Polio. (My cousin Jackie's legs are encased in cumbersome braces; she needs crutches to walk.)

Goiters. (Just the word makes me squeamish. I'm not entirely clear on what this condition is but have overheard talk. I picture a growth swinging from my neck, like an udder.)

Rusty nails.

Cow horns and hoofs. (Our father has told us cautionary tales of carelessness. Grown men kicked senseless. Gored. I have nightmares.)

As we sit on the fence, arguing, an insect dips close, its wings as gossamer and filmy as the gauze my mother used to make our angel costumes for the church school Christmas pageant. It is a dragonfly, an insect we know as the Devil's Darning Needle. Somewhere we've heard that if you are sleeping, it can seal your eyes. If you're awake, it can stitch your lips shut. I am too old to believe this myth, but still I duck my head and cover my mouth.

Sandy follows its progress as it flits off across the pasture. "Just think," she says. "If one sewed up your mouth, you couldn't eat."

"Worse," I say, "you couldn't speak." It seems to me that nothing could be more punishing than to be stripped of my voice, to be struck mute, imprisoned in a wordless world. Helen Keller before Annie Sullivan.

Although I enjoy solitude of my own design, and pass hours and hours exploring fields and woods with Lady at my side, the child I am rankles against imposed rules of stillness. At school, I am constantly in trouble for talking in the classroom. The Conduct box on my report card is usually marked *U* for "Unsatisfactory," and the constant theme of my parent-teacher conferences is that I disrupt the class with my chatter. Could I have this fierce anxiety about being silenced because censorship has already begun?

Don't say that. It isn't nice.

Don't interrupt.

Lower your voice.

Don't talk in class.

Children should be seen and not heard.

Don't tell.

Don't laugh so loud. The other girls won't like you.

The girl I am can no more imagine growing into a woman who deliberately practices silence than she can picture one of the Holsteins flying up to dance the two-step atop the silo's dome.

Like the Roman god Janus, silence holds two faces. To be silenced is not at all the same as choosing not to speak. A chasm lies between the two, as wide as that between fasting for a purpose and starvation. To be silenced is crippling, belittling, constricting, disempowering. Chosen stillness can be healing, expansive, instructive.

How do we reconcile these silences? How do we sort out the intentions behind them? How do we find ways to use stillness as a means of connecting to our deepest beings and to others? To finding the genuine in ourselves?

How can we come to understand why silence is sometimes sacred and other times profane?

My friends have not been imprisoned like Reza Daneshvar, but many have shared with me experiences of how they were stripped of their voices. One told me her niece's boyfriend had murdered someone and the family's position was that it should never be spoken of again, as if, ignored, this horrific fact could be made to disappear. Another friend grew up in a family of great abuse—substance and sexual—and spoke about the silence that surrounded both, how it wove a web of complicity that trapped the entire family and perpetuated secrets.

In her book *After Silence*, Nancy Venable Raine writes movingly about the years following her rape, how during that time she kept still and how that silence held "the rusty taste of shame."

Shame is not the only thing that can rob us of speech. Cultural taboos foster silence. Criticism, judgment, and sarcasm are all effective at muting our voices. As are ridicule and rejection. We don't want to be thought wrong or different, and so we keep still. It can feel unsafe to express our deepest feelings and independent thoughts. We can be censored and we can censor ourselves. Being silenced, whether externally or internally, means being cut off from our genuine selves. Our institutions, too, have many ways of silencing us, as anyone who has been minimized by a teacher knows.

One day I was invited to speak to a second-grade class about writing. I began by talking about the importance for writers of not being afraid to speak up. It is the first prerequisite, I told the class. And then, as a warm-up exercise, I asked them to make the sound of their favorite animal. Within seconds the room erupted. Hoots, howls, barks, meows, baas. And within minutes, they were at their desks writing a story about their animal, beginning with the premise, "What if . . ."

One child wrote, "What if a tiger kept a human for a pet?"

I was struck by one thing that morning: Unlike many older students, not one child resisted writing a story. No one disclaimed that she was better at math or that he was better at soccer and wasn't good at English. Watching them, I was reminded of a study out of the University of Michigan that Madeleine L'Engle wrote of in her book *Walking on Water*. The study found that in first grade the students asked 80 percent of the questions, by fifth grade they asked 50 percent, and in high school only 20 percent, the rest instead coming from the teachers. Somehow, in the first eight years of school, students learned not to ask questions, to be silenced.

The evening after I spoke to the second graders, I gave a talk to an audience of three hundred adults. Still inspired by the morning's experience with the children, I decided on the spot to duplicate the exercise. Again I spoke about the importance for writers of not being afraid to use their voices. And then I asked everyone in the audience to make the sound of their favorite animal. I was greeted by a silence so complete it felt as if everyone had stopped breathing. I understood. It was too risky. Many of us are afraid we'll be the only one barking like a dog, screeching like an owl.

But just as imposed silence can shut us down from creativity, spontaneity, and the deepest truths of our genuine being, I was discovering the glorious paradox that deliberately claimed silence could serve as the bridge to finding my authentic self. It was silence, after all, that was leading me back to my center and serving as a path to empowerment and self-knowledge. I was no longer a girl sitting on a fence, afraid of an insect that could sew her lips closed. I now understood the difference between being silenced and claiming silence.

And so I began to collect dragonflies. Silver and stained glass and brass. Needlepoint and paper. Pins and earrings and charms. All symbols to remind me that I should not be prevented from speaking my truths.

In silence I had found a place where I could hear the voice inside.

I could sit in the sun and sip the sweetness of its cup.

I slowed down, reflected, and rested. And I wanted more.

CHAPTER 7

Boneyard

Surrendering
THE *Need* TO BE *Right*

"SO CAN YOU TELL your wife off on Mondays?" another fisherman asked Hillary one day.

"Yeah, but I better be out of town on Tuesday," he replied.

It is an early June day in the third year of my silent Mondays. Hillary and I are driving along Old King's Highway, a road that meanders along the north side of Cape Cod. Originally a stagecoach route, it stretches from Sandwich to Provincetown and is one of the most scenic of the Cape's roads. This day holds the promise of the coming summer. The air is heavy with the fragrance of lilacs blooming in the gardens of old farmsteads and in the yards of sea captains' mansions and white clapboard colonials built centuries ago.

The day before was the last of five days of double tides for Hillary. These occur each month at the full and the new moons and mean that twice each day the tide recedes low enough to harvest shellfish. In the winter there is not enough daylight to fish the very early and late tides, but in the spring and throughout the summer Hillary rises at 4:00 a.m., harvests quahogs for four hours, and then returns in the late afternoon to fish the second tide. This dictates that sometimes—especially if there's been a Red Sox game on the West Coast the night before—he may sleep as little as four or five hours. This particular afternoon, I glance over and see how tired he is and my heart fills with a protective tenderness. *He looks exhausted. I wish I could fish for him. He works too hard.*

Then, out of nowhere, he mentions a petty complaint, something I have neglected to do, although he has asked me several times. I shoot a look at him, but, oblivious, he continues on, finding fault.

Not talking, I am unable to defend myself. I feel attacked. Has he deliberately brought up the reproof because I can't respond? How unfair of him to choose this day to voice his criticism. As quickly as, only instants before, it opened to him, my heart claps shut. My appreciation for him, for the scenery, for the day evaporates.

And he keeps talking. Armed with my own list of grievances, I am now deaf. And storing ammunition. *Don't think this is the end of it*, I fume. *Just wait until tomorrow. You can bet we'll be discussing this.*

As I cultivate my arguments I find myself getting more

resentful, the relaxed and sweet mood of the drive completely shattered. My mouth may be silent, but my mind is in overdrive, working up righteous indignation. I'm not listening to Hillary; I'm not even listening to myself. Just because I've proclaimed a day of silence does not necessarily mean I am serene or even quiet. We bring to the table what we bring to the table.

After we return to the house, my foul mood hangs on, tainting the day. I counsel myself to let it go, to take a walk to the beach.

"Want company?" Hillary asks, as I head out.

I shake my head. In spite of my intention to surrender it, I cling to my resentment like a junkyard hound with a ham hock. I have my own bone to pick with Hillary.

At the shore, the tide is out. The afternoon sun softens the light on the grasses. I walk over the wooden bridge that spans the clam flat and sit, drawing my knees up and circling my legs with my arms. A few feet away in the mud, I see a large, three-toed claw print that looks nearly pterodactyl. I hear a hoarse, guttural squawk and look up to see the slow flapping of pearly wings as a great blue heron takes flight over the marsh. With its six-foot wingspan and neck S-shaped in flight it resembles a flying dinosaur.

Normally, the sight of these birds awakens wonder, but not this day. Given the opportunity to connect with the majesty of nature, I squander it. I am too caught up with defending my ego and too preoccupied with lugging my resentment around like a sack of skeletons, both heavy and useless. I am like the first monk in one of my favorite Buddhist parables.

. . .

Two monks, as part of their vows, have promised never again to touch a woman. One day, while walking, they come to the edge of a river, where an astonishingly beautiful woman stands. Unable to cross unaided, she asks the monks for help. The first monk refuses, explaining that to help her would require that he break a solemn oath. The second monk reflects a moment and then picks the woman up and carries her across the stream. Once safely across, he sets her down. The two monks continue on their way.

As the hours pass, the first monk grows more and more agitated. Finally, unable to remain silent, he turns to the other monk and says, "I can't go on without speaking to you of something."

"What is it?"

"You and I both took an oath never to touch a woman as long as we lived."

"It is true. We did."

"But back there at the river, you carried the woman across."

"Yes," the second monk replies.

"So you broke your sacred vow."

"Well, it is true, I did carry the woman across the river, but then I put her down," the monk says. "You have been carrying her ever since."

.   .   .

When I first read this little story, I was struck by its inherent truth. It is not the burdens and resentments we pick up that keep us derailed, but our *continuing* to tote them. I *know* this—even as I turn to leave the beach—but like that first monk, I am unwilling to set my resentment down. The sour taste of it remains even after I return from the beach, and I retreat from Hillary for the remainder of the day. Our tools can only serve the purpose we put them to. In the past, silence has served me well, but this day its usefulness is clouded by my resentment and it does not provide a refuge. Instead it has become a crucible in which to stoke my discontent. I *know* what is going on, what I need to release, but still I carry the bones. Hillary is not the only stubborn one in the family.

When I wake the next morning I glance over at him.

"Good morning, Sunshine," he says.

"Morning." Once, months before, I had a dream in which he had betrayed me. On waking, I'd been hurt and annoyed, and, even though it had only been a dream, it had taken a while to release these feelings. I feel the same way now. I am irritated with him but don't know why. Had I had another dream?

"How was your day of silence?" he asks.

"Good," I say. I turn away slightly.

"Anything wrong?"

"No." And then I remember our drive along the highway. The maddening thing is I can recall the drive, but not the specifics of the comment that lit the firestorm in me.

"You sure? You seem a little funny."

"No," I say again. "I just have a lot on my mind." How angry I had been with him. Infuriated, really. I can recall my ranting mind, my escape to the beach. I just can't remember the exact words that set me off. I can hardly ask him. He might be stubborn but he isn't stupid.

"Coffee?" he asks.

"Okay."

After he goes down to the kitchen, I lie in bed, trying to dredge up some fragment of his comment from yesterday. What had he said that had so upset me?

But no matter how hard I try, I can't remember. Can. Not. Remember. As I lie there I marvel that a remark that had pulled me both from serenity and from myself had been so minor, so insignificant that I am unable to recall it less than twenty-four hours later.

And then I wonder this: What if it hadn't been a silent day? If I had been speaking during our drive, where would our discussion have led? And to what purpose?

Knee-jerk reactions. Automatic responses. Spontaneous eruptions. How many times do we jump into an argument, eager as a bluefish striking a glittery lure, when if we waited a day, an hour, our words would be tempered? How often do we offer advice when what is really required is a compassionate ear?

Arsenius, one of the early Christian Desert Fathers, said, "I have often repented of having spoken, but never of having kept silent." And the Algonquin have a saying: "Talk is talk. Silence is wisdom." How do we come to this intelligence? How do we incorporate it in our lives?

When we are truly silent—within and without—we surrender the ego's need to be right. This is sometimes difficult. Many of us have learned that to be wrong is to be shamed, to be less than, to be judged and found wanting. We fear not being loved or accepted.

Given a choice, of course we would rather be right than be wrong. But, as I was that day with Hillary, too often we would rather be right than be happy. Or even content.

On that day driving along the north shore of the Cape, I was learning that silence can be invaluable in providing time and space to defuse a situation. Its surrounds can provide a neutral corner in which to sit, an opportunity to reflect rather than react. It can help break patterns of habitual behavior. It is a quiet well into which we can gaze deeply. And, like a well, it offers us a reflection of ourselves, but a reflection in reverse so we can glimpse something unexpected. It is a deep resource from which we can draw the most vital water to nourish ourselves.

Chuang Tzu wrote, "Men do not mirror themselves in running water—they mirror themselves in still water. Only what is still can still the stillness of other things."

In the months after that day with Hillary, I learned

more of the lessons of silence—how to choose speech mindfully and truly listen both to myself and to others. On my silent days, I was being challenged to release illusions about myself. As I looked more deeply at my intentions, reactions, and responses, I could observe myself as I truly was. My generosities and miserliness. My impulses to withhold or to give. My fears and regrets. And through observing, I could connect to new levels of inner truth. Like the ancient mystics, I was learning that it was by going into the desert that inner strength emerged.

As the months and years passed, I rediscovered that silence was not a product but a *process*, one that often pulled me from mindless behavior and offered opportunities for transformation. In fact, each silent Monday continued to bring a new teaching, a fresh crop of understanding.

But on the day Hillary and I rode along Old King's Highway, silence's gift was to save me from my foolish, pride-filled self. Stillness had given me an opportunity to relinquish what was not important. To receive rather than resist. Whatever the gift that was being given.

So from that day on was I enlightened? Perfect? My responses always reasoned? Kind?

Boneyard

Oh, if it were only that easy. Oh, that our life teachings were set on a linear path, or even a curved arc, instead of a spiral. On this circular journey I would encounter the same lessons again and again. But silence remained my ever-patient teacher.

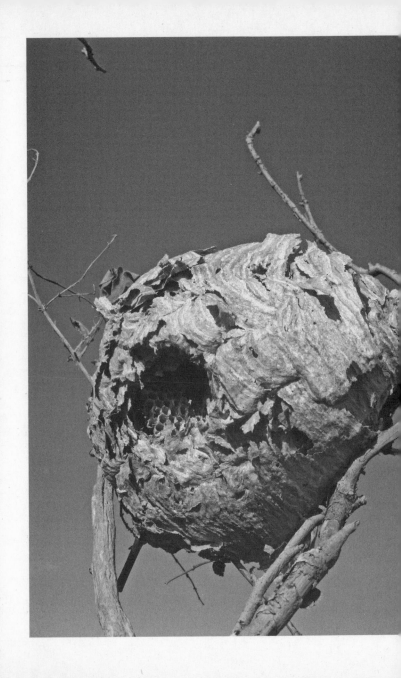

CHAPTER 8

Bees

Choosing the Right Words

NOT TOO LONG AFTER that day with Hillary, I answered the phone and heard our daughter's voice.

"I'm so exhausted," Hope said. "I only got three hours of sleep last night and I have eight clients today."

I didn't miss a beat. Instantly I began a litany of the things she needed to do to take care of herself.

When she spoke again, I heard the tears in her voice. "I don't want to be told what I *should* be doing," she said. "I just want someone to listen."

· · ·

And so I still found myself falling into old patterns. Speaking foolishly or without reflection or sensitivity. I still allowed myself to be drawn into needless arguments, and I continued to offer advice and counsel where none had been sought. This was particularly true when I held strong opinions or in areas I felt I had expertise. As if what I had to say was more important. Okay, let's be frank, in areas where I felt I knew it all. And despite my best intentions, I still wounded others with thoughtless, ill-considered speech.

But as I entered the garden of silence again and again, seeds of awareness were growing. Continually, stillness slowed me and made me pay attention. I grew more mindful of language. I made a commitment to slow down and learn to listen. And so on days of silence, I would listen more intently to what others said. And to my own mental chatter. I heard nuances more clearly and observed body language more acutely.

In stillness, I could hear in my mind the echo of the words I would have said if I had been speaking and so was able to observe my habitual responses and behaviors—such as my tendency to interrupt or to finish others' sentences. In silence, I could contemplate them with detachment. And I would hear reflected in others' conversations the echo of my own, the expressions of concern and love and gratitude as well as the petty complaints, tiresome dramas, and mean-spirited observations, the exaggerations and boastfulness. And I saw how clearly we are revealed by our speech.

And I vowed to do better.

And failed. Time and again.

But failed with growing awareness.

A silent Monday is a good day to be considering language. As I write this I am sitting in a writing studio at the Virginia Center for the Creative Arts, an artists' retreat on the lip of the Blue Ridge Mountains. It is early April and the redbud, dogwood, and flowering pear are in full bloom, their scent lacing the air, creamy and seductive. In response, immense bees have appeared. They circle outside my studio's screen door, buzzing in a frenzy of intoxication. They are huge—large enough to use as badminton shuttlecocks—and their song is as oversized as they are. So much noise for creatures who, like snakes, starfish, and snails, are completely deaf.

As I watch them, I think of how they can both sting and make honey.

Like words.

In nearby studios, poets are using language to shape verse and novelists to craft stories and tell truths. At this moment, across the planet, others, too, are creating with words. Or using them as instruments of slander or punishment.

Just as a blade can pare fruit, sculpt wood, or inflict injury, or a key can set free or imprison, in hundreds of tongues around the world, words are being employed both to hurt and to heal. To cause both peace and chaos. To connect and to isolate. To praise and to condemn. Create harmony and discord. Honor and abase. To mask truth and to tell it. To align and to alienate neighbors and nations.

Again I consider, how do I use my allotment? How mindful am I of my intent? How responsible am I to my speech? How long will the effects of my carelessly spoken words linger? In silence, I sit and contemplate.

Bees

There is a book called *The Hidden Messages of Water* by the Japanese scientist Dr. Masaru Emoto. When Dr. Emoto began experimenting with photographing ice crystals, he found that when the water he used for the experiments was exposed to words like "love" and "gratitude" and "wisdom," it formed stunningly beautiful crystals. But when it was subjected to words like "hate" and "You're ugly," the crystals became dark, malformed, and fragmented.

Earlier this morning, as I stared at the photographs Dr. Emoto took—visual evidence of the power of language—I wondered this: If the vibrations of words can affect water so dramatically, what do they do to us? We who are comprised of more than 70 percent water.

"Our emotions and feelings have an effect on the world moment by moment," Dr. Emoto writes. "If you send out words and images of creativity, then you will be contributing to the creation of a beautiful world. However, emitting messages of destruction, you contribute to the destruction of the universe."

I don't need to look at history or headlines to know the truth of this. Or even the stunning proof of Emoto's photographs. I only need to examine my own life. The times I've harmed with words and the times I have been hurt.

In college some of the women in my dorm would occasionally hold "truth" nights. In these sessions we would select one coed and tell her what about her needed improving, an exercise far more mean-spirited than helpful. How long did the effects of these nights last? How much hurt did we create in each other's hearts?

.   .   .

A story. A young girl is walking home from sixth grade. She carries an armload of books, a heart full of worries. On the opposite sidewalk, other classmates walk. One, a boy, yells over to her, "Hey, Dreamboat."

She turns, smiling, her spirits momentarily lifted.

"Not you, Shipwreck," he shouts. His friends laugh. Shame stains the girl's face.

A cruel joke, carelessly spoken and no doubt long forgotten by the boy who hurled it. But not by the girl. Even now, decades later, I can remember the sting of those words. How they struck my body as swift and sure as a blow.

Sticks and stones may break my bones, but words can never hurt me.

So facile, these words meant to console us after schoolyard taunts. But not true. Not true.

Words are the seeds we plant in the earth of our days.

You don't have to be a farmer to know that if you plant a turnip you won't grow a gardenia.

One early March evening, I stood in front of the deli counter at the local market. The only other customer was an older woman with two young children in tow, a girl of about seven and a boy of about four. I listened as she chastised them and threatened them, telling the boy if he didn't behave she would call the police and they would take him away.

Usually when I witness anyone yelling or threatening children, I sit in judgment, all huffy and self-righteous, and cast disapproving looks through narrowed eyes. In a moment I later recognized as one touched by grace, instead of glaring, for some reason on this day I smiled at the woman. "Kids can be a handful," I said. "But you have two beautiful children."

Her face softened. "Yes, they are," she said. She reached out to stroke the girl's dark hair.

Within minutes, she was telling me that she was their grandmother, that she had a full-time job and took care of the children evenings while her daughter worked. She was exhausted. But she was no longer angry. The boy and girl, too, had quieted.

A simple thing. A momentary exchange between two

strangers. It stayed with me for years because it was such a vivid example of how a kind response can change everything. If I had not been schooled by silence, would my reaction have been my usual one, formed by mindless, judgmental habit?

Another story. A young woman is living across the country when she hears the news of her beloved grandfather's death. *How old was he? Ninety-five? Well, he had a good long life,* a coworker tells her. A second colleague mentions heaven. These sentiments bounce off her like rain on drought-hardened clay, for no matter how long a person lives, or what our religious beliefs are, death is a loss.

Then a man pulls a chair up to her desk, sits, and takes her hand. "Tell me about your grandfather," he says. The girl begins to talk.

Ralph Waldo Emerson wrote, "Let us become silent that we may hear the whispers of the gods . . . and by lowly listening we shall hear the right word."

The right words.

Finding them requires attention. It calls for us to stop spouting the easy clichés and banalities, to ask beyond the obvious, or to cease looking for them and simply listen. Again and again people who have experienced grief say that they have found comfort beyond speech in the attentive, quiet listening of friends.

I recently read about a woman undergoing chemotherapy. She said friends just didn't know what to say to her. One person said, "This is your wake-up call."

The woman was furious, the comment implying that her life had required a wake-up call.

The late mime and master of silence Marcel Marceau said, "Do not the most moving moments in our life find us without words?"

The trouble is, not knowing what to say, too often we say something anyway.

.   .   .

I think, too, about how words can obscure real feeling and connection between people, and then between people and the greater cosmos. As Dr. Daniel Siegel wrote in an article in the November 2006 issue of *Psychotherapy Networker*, "Our ordinary language can be a prison, locking us in the jail of our own redundancies, dulling our senses, clouding our focus."

My friend, the author Eleanor Morse, who lives on an island off the coast of Maine, traveled to India. She found that the silence that happened naturally when people tried to communicate in an unfamiliar language created a deeper connection than she was accustomed to.

When she returned home, Eleanor was struck by the

richness of feeling in the e-mails she received from her new friends. "They were so present," she said. "Here's an example: 'You have told me about your Island I never been any Island even never saw the Sea, So when I emagin of Sea and Island I fill with joy.' "

One person wrote, "Enjoy the life it never come back."

Enjoy the life it never come back has now become a kind of incantation for Eleanor.

When we are facile in a language, we tend to fling words like a spendthrift with deep pockets rather than use them with precision. What would happen if we listened to our own language as if it were a foreign tongue? What if we had to search for our words? And speak them as slowly and responsibly?

.   .   .

There is another Buddhist parable that is pertinent here.

A young nun joins an order in which she must take a vow of silence. Once a year, on her birthday, each nun is allowed to speak briefly.

The first year, the young nun meets with the abbess, who asks if there is anything she wants to say.

"Yes," says the young nun. "My bed is too hard."

Another year passes. Again the nun goes for her audience with the abbess, who again asks if there is anything she would like to say.

"Yes," the nun says. "The food here is terrible."

Another year passes. This time when the abbess asks if there is anything she would like to say, the nun responds, "Yes, I'm leaving."

"I'm not surprised," the abbess replies. "Ever since you got here, you've done nothing but complain."

How do we use our allotment?

Like soil, fertilized and turned over, silence was becoming richer with each passing Monday, each passing year. More than scripture readings or sermons, it was making me conscious of my choices, both of words and of actions. Repeatedly, because of forced contemplation, it tutored me in responsible speech.

The Sufis say that, if we are to speak well, our words must pass three gates. At the first gate we ask: *Are these words true?* At the second: *Are they necessary?* At the third: *Are they kind?*

"Truth without kindness is cruelty," a wise man named Saul once told me.

Silence created new awareness. It provided a space that allowed me to think about what I was saying, to hear my words in the echo chamber of my mind, and to find both my truths and the kindness with which to tell them.

CHAPTER 9

Birdsong

Learning THE *Difference*
BETWEEN *Listening* AND
Waiting TO *Talk*

WHEN SHE FIRST ARRIVED at her uncle's estate and was exploring the grounds, Mary Lennox caught sight of a bird with a bright red breast sitting on the topmost branch of a tree, "and suddenly he burst into his winter song—almost as if he had caught sight of her and was calling to her."

On one particular morning my friend Ann and I were sitting in her backyard, which is bordered by woods. Suddenly Ann leaned forward, her body as poised as a hunting dog in point.

"Listen," she whispered.

"What?" I concentrated.

Ann cocked her head. Her face was lit with delight. "Carolina wren," she said.

From the woods, I heard the call. Three clear syllables. *Tee-ka-lah. Tee-ka-lah. Tee-ka-lah.*

"What I love about the Carolina wren," Ann said, "is that for such a small bird, it has such a loud song."

I have always been amazed that, like music lovers who can identify the composer after hearing only the opening bars of a sonata, serious bird-watchers can identify so many

different birds by their songs. To distinguish subtleties—
whether of music or birdcall—requires both stillness and
the careful and attentive listening that is a form of love.
Are we our own bird-watchers? How do we learn to recognize our own calls? How long do we have to wait to
recognize all the songs? And like Mary's robin, could they
be calling to us?

Life-birds. That is what birders call birds they see for
the very first time. Could we hear our own life-birds if we
learned to listen?

And how would the world change if we did?

The discipline of silence was leading me not only to a
keener attention to language but to an improved capacity for
hearing. On silent Mondays, I began to listen differently—
to myself, to others, and to the world around me.

It was a listening I would call both active and without
an agenda.

I discovered how often, in silence, I heard the echo of
what I would have said if I had been talking. I was surprised
at how frequently I was frustrated because I couldn't offer
my opinions. And, of course, busy with my own thoughts, I
realized that I wasn't fully listening to others.

But gradually, as Mondays came and went, I began
to observe that when there was no expectation for me to

respond, to acknowledge, analyze, disagree, or otherwise comment, I listened differently. My ego relaxed. With the distance and space that silence provided, I was able to recognize the motivations and intents beneath my unspoken words, and I was more receptive to the ideas and opinions of others.

Of course, conversation can stimulate, inform, and build strong connections. It can be the thread that weaves us together and binds us to our tribe. At best it can inspire, comfort, motivate, and kindle creative thought. But as I listened more carefully I discovered that much of the dialogue in our culture is what someone once called "talking and waiting to talk." We engage in chatter, not conversation, and our chatter reveals our egos' needs: Love me, admire me, envy me, fear me, help me, see me. There is little space for truly hearing others.

In silence I was hearing others more keenly and witnessing my own thoughts, too, and seeing how they served to separate or to connect me. I was learning not to turn away from the parts of myself that were difficult.

. . .

In the fifth year of my practice, I was again a resident at the Ragdale Foundation in northern Illinois. The first evening of my stay, I entered the dining room and placed my "I Am Having a Day of Silence" card in front of one place at the table. Others came into the room, chose seats.

The buzz of conversation filled the air. Wineglasses were filled. The chef set out food on the sideboard. Plates piled high, we all sat down and then, at the suggestion of the director, we went around the table and the other fellows took turns telling where they were from and what their discipline was.

I didn't know any of the other residents and was growing more and more anxious about being in silence. Were they judging me? Not speaking, had I become invisible? The thought made me uncomfortable, pricked my ego.

I listened as one after another told about himself. Without even being aware of it, I slipped into critical mind. One person was boastful. Another authoritative. Still another boring. And a fourth dominated the conversation. I was not speaking, but my mind was busy—impatient, disapproving. Once again, I was so busy judging, I was unable to hear. I was separated from my fellow artists not only by my silence, but by my own insecurities, which had engendered a need to be superior, so very often the place out of which judgment is born.

But after a while, my silence created a space around me

and my anxiety eased. While the hum of conversation continued, I withdrew to the safe place of inner stillness. My mind quieted. The spinning of the world slowed. And then I began to watch myself watching others. I saw how, to validate my own ego, I judged others.

When I again tuned in to the talk at the table, a major shift had occurred. As if something had cracked open inside my chest, I was overcome with waves of tenderness toward the people I had been judging only moments earlier. I saw how, in this noisy world, we shout so to be heard.

Instead of the actual words spoken at that table, I heard the desires and needs beneath them and was softened with empathy. I understood. The painter listing all the galleries where she had shown her work, the composer who interrupted a writer to talk about his new opera, the writer who talked on and on about being on *Oprah*, the novelist whose book had just been sold to the movies—like any of us, all each wanted was to be seen and heard and validated.

Silence brought me to a place of kindness and compassion. Sitting in silence, we are given an opportunity to develop sensitivity, compassion, and empathy. In stillness, we can develop the discipline that is required to listen fully.

.   .   .

Birdsong

The American philosopher Eugene Kennedy wrote, "There is a silence that matches our best possibilities when we have learned to listen to others. We can master the art of being quiet in order to be able to hear clearly what others are saying. . . . We need to cut off the garbled static of our own preoccupations to give to people who want our quiet attention."

I love Kennedy's phrase "a silence that matches our best possibilities."

This kind of quiet is also necessary in order to hear our own inner voice. Our own birdsong.

My friend Dr. John Clark, a former professor of medieval literature, became a life coach after retiring from his university job. A crucial skill required in coaching is the ability to listen. He told me that during his training, his adviser told him there are four kinds of listening:

> *Listening but not hearing.*
>
> *Listening and connecting with one's own agenda.*
>
> *Listening and hearing without a personal agenda.*
>
> *Intuitive listening, meaning not only hearing what is being spoken but what is not being said. Deep listening.*

Listening but not hearing. Haven't we all done that? Been present in body but not in mind? Sat while someone chatted on, preoccupied with our own thoughts, what we have left to do in the day, looking ahead to what we have to do tomorrow, pretending to listen. Margaret calls that "giving radio time." And at one time or another, haven't we also been on the other side of that situation, aware while we are talking that we don't have the other's attention, even if the person is wearing a "listening face"?

Listening and connecting with one's own agenda. This means talking and waiting to talk. While another is speaking, we're rehearsing our response. A mother readying her argument that vegetables are good for him even while her son is stating his dislike of beets. The woman waiting out her friend's tale of a romance gone bad so she can soothe the hurt by saying the man was a rat and that she's better off without him. Cutting short someone's grief with facile words of condolence because we find the sorrow too painful to hear.

Listening and hearing without a personal agenda. A woman who was grieving following the death of her son said that the most helpful of all the people who came to console her after the accident was an older woman. "She just sat with me, held my hand. She listened to everything. My grief, despair, guilt, anger. All of it without speaking. On that day, her silent listening was more helpful than a thousand words of consolation." In listening this way, we bear witness for one another. My friend Ginny says this is true when we share the details of illness as well. "We don't want solutions," she says. "Just a sympathetic ear."

Intuitive listening. Hearing what is not being said. This listening is a gift. It is listening with heart. It is what the most skillful and compassionate of therapists are capable of. And good parents. It is a mother knowing that when her daughter says she doesn't want to go to a party, she is ashamed about being overweight. It is when an older parent says, "I don't need help," and her middle-aged son knows that what she is really saying is, "I don't want to be a burden."

The first Rule of St. Benedict is this: Listen.

To be truly heard is to be understood. It is a central longing of our souls. To listen, says Paul Tillich, is the first duty of love. And the writer Rachel Naomi Remen writes, "The most basic and powerful way to connect to another person is to listen. Just listen. Perhaps the most important thing we ever give each other is our attention. . . . A loving silence often has far more power to heal and to connect than the most well intentioned words."

A gardener once told me that when he is completely silent in his garden he is able to hear the sound of a seedling breaking through the ground. How quiet do we have to be to hear the plant sprouting, the Carolina wren in the woods, and the small birdsong deep inside ourselves? This is the voice theologians and philosophers and poets have called the voice of God.

"Silence," wrote Herman Melville, "is the one and only voice of God."

What is it trying to tell us?

In order to follow inner wisdom, we have to first know it. In order to know it, we have to hear it; to hear it, we have to be still.

Habits are so deeply ingrained that in spite of best intentions, we fall back into mindless behavior. It is stopping and paying attention that awakens us.

I still have on my desk the conch shell I picked up at the beach on my second day of silence. *Listen,* it continues to remind me. *Listen to what you can hear when you are being still.*

PART THREE

Fertilization

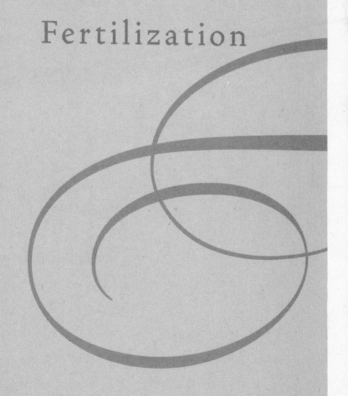

CHAPTER 10

Spiderweb

Nourishing
THE *Creative Self*

HILLARY APPEARS at the studio door. "I'm going to the post office," he says. "Do you need me to pick up anything?"

I'm unable to suppress a sigh. My train of thought, ephemeral as a windblown waft of mayflower, is gone.

"What?" he says.

"That's the third time in ten minutes you've interrupted me," I say. We've had this conversation before.

"I wasn't bothering you," he replies. "I only was telling you I was going to get the mail."

I read the words on the screen in front of me, trying to recapture the elusive thought, but it is gone. Gone. Gone. Gone.

. . .

Henri Matisse once said, "Whoever wishes to devote himself to painting should begin by cutting out his tongue."

Or someone else's.

Okay, severing a tongue does seem a *wee* bit dramatic, but Matisse is absolutely right, in that creativity requires silence in which to flourish.

Spiderweb

It is the first essential. And it is a challenge to deliberately carve out such stillness.

We need water of stillness with which to nourish our creative selves. Repeatedly, artists, writers, scientists, and philosophers have written of this need, not only for the process of creating but within the work itself.

Just as a seed is first nourished in the dark and silent depths of earth, creativity always begins in the void: the empty canvas, the blank page. Springing out of and weaving through this emptiness blossoms art, music, poetry, literature. In the clearing we discover possibilities.

I try to imagine any art form without silence, but find it impossible. A garden needs room between rows, between plantings. Paintings require negative space. Music needs the Grand Pause. Poetry needs line breaks. Try and picture a page of prose without margins and indentations and breaks between words. The eye rejects it. Without silence, however it is imposed, art becomes chaotic, a confusing jumble without order or meaning.

From the very first silent Monday I was struck by how much more fruitful my studio time was on these days. When not pulled into communication with the external world, I was able to enter the sphere of my work more completely, to go deeper, to develop abstract thought. With fewer external diversions—even those as minor as a phone call or Hillary coming in to say he was off on an errand—ideas were more accessible and flowed more easily. As new insights rose from the subconscious, connections were made, problems solved. And fleeting thoughts were allowed to alight.

But it was more than the excising of external demands and the obvious effect of not being fragmented that sparked my creativity on these days. Stillness centered me and allowed me to focus. I'm reminded again of my first silent day and the analogy of the ear trumpet that came to me in the shower, how we live with one ear turned out to the world and how everything changes when both ears are turned inward. This kind of attention to our work—complete and without interruption, an undistracted concentration—enables us to tap into a groundwater of creativity not readily available when our attention is fractured.

The Virginia artist Cleveland Morris paints canvases that are powerful in their simplicity and clarity.

"Still life requires stillness," he says. "The word 'still' is in there for a reason. You find a quiet that is a harmony. A sound that is a great openness. It asks of the painter a fearlessness to go into the silence. A great still-life painting stops you in your tracks because you want to be still, to enter a great tunnel."

Spiderweb

I once asked Cleveland if he needs absolute quiet in his studio. He replied that while he sometimes listens to music, he turns it off at a critical point in the painting process. "I don't think art is possible without silence," he said. "The ultimate spiritual discovery is in silence, not in noise. Hearing what there is to hear without detritus. We have to hear our own soundtrack and we can only hear that in the silence within."

Musicians are particularly articulate on the importance of silence, both in the process and in the score. "The notes I handle no better than many pianists," said the musician Artur Schnabel. "But the pauses between the notes—ah, that is where art resides."

My friend Jane Lowey told me, "My work with music and choral directing has taught me the deepest respect for the emptiness between the notes. Of course, there is no music without the silence. It is silence that actually gives life to sound. Sometimes I think of the choral work as 'the voice, the circle, and silence.'"

"In a score, *Morendo al niente* means a fading away to nothing," the composer Stephen Dankner explains. "It is used to clear the air, to distinguish one section from another."

A team of scientists from Stanford and McGill universities watched brain images of eighteen volunteers who listened to a series of movements within symphonies, each punctuated by frequent pauses. They found that a one- to two-second break between movements triggers a flurry of mental activity in the brain. When the music resumes, the action shifts to a different part of the brain, then subsides. This suggests that important work is being done in the space of silence.

"The pause itself becomes the event," said neuroscientist Vinod Menon of Stanford's School of Medicine, the senior author of the study's paper. "A pause is not a time when nothing happens."

Again and again on silent days, I was discovering the truth of this. Silence was not an emptiness, but a time of rich meaning and a place where much work got done.

One day, while walking through the Boston Garden, I was drawn to the statue of Mary Dyer, a Quaker who was hanged on Boston Commons in 1660. Against the clamor of city life, I was struck by the simplicity of the sculpture's lines, the serene clarity in the work. I looked up information about the sculptor, Sylvia Shaw Judson, and learned that she, like Dyer, was a Quaker, a person whose worship centers on silence. In the introduction to a small book of her work, Judson wrote, "I was once impressed by seeing slides of sick blood cells and healthy blood cells. The sick cells looked diffused and scattered; the healthy cells had an organized center and pattern. I deeply believe that a work of art as well as life is better for a coherent design."

Silence provides the space that defines and gives organized shape to our compositions and our days.

.   .   .

One late August afternoon, after he'd finished mowing the lawn, Hillary poured himself a glass of chardonnay and sat in a wicker chair on the front porch. Too late to initiate a new project, too early to think about starting dinner, it was that lovely, languid hour that calls for one to pause.

I don't know how long he stayed there, but the sun had set when he finally came in. He found me in the studio.

"It was beautiful out there," he said. "I watched a catbird in the birdbath."

"Nice," I said, absorbed in the work at hand.

"And a cardinal came and perched on the edge of the porch. It practically flew into my lap."

"Nice," I parroted, still inattentive.

And then he said something that pulled me from my preoccupation and rang with wisdom.

"If you can sit still," he said, "so much comes to you."

If we can sit still. That is the trick. Animals know this.

And hunters and naturalists. And artists. All recognize the importance of holding quiet, of observing. Imagination requires its quiet roosting space. Like the solitary spider who busily weaves her web in perfect silence, we need to be alone and quiet for our subconscious to spin its creations. Stillness focuses the brain. And like the tensile strength of the spider's strands, it buttresses and strengthens creativity.

René Marois, a neuroscientist and director of the Human Information and Processing Laboratory at Vanderbilt University, conducted research designed to measure how much efficiency is lost when subjects tried to handle more than one task at a time. "A core limitation," he found about the human brain, "is an inability to concentrate on two things at once."

No matter how we speak of multitasking, the brain is essentially capable of paying whole attention to only one single thing. And whole attention is what is required in creating. It is a form of love.

In the cacophony of modern life, we forget this. We forget that stillness is not only supportive of the creative process but is its necessary underpinning. We forget, that is, until a moment when our complete concentration is required. Then, like the artist Cleveland Morris, we turn off distractions. This is why the golfer tees his ball in absolute silence. And why, when trying to find our way in an unfamiliar city, we turn off the car radio. And why, at artists' colonies, the one inviolate rule is that fellows cannot be disturbed while working in their studios. (Once, while in residence at the Virginia Center for the Creative Arts, a painter kept knocking on the studio door of the writer A. Manette Ansay. Finally, Ansay posted a sign on her door: "DO NOT DISTURB. Under any conditions. Even fire. If the building burns down and I go with it, it is my own damn fault.")

Today our imaginations are under siege by a constant barrage of noise and busyness. Our culture regards solitude and silence as something to be avoided. We would rather scrub grout than spend extended time alone.

A high cost comes with this. We have lost the path by which we journey to the place deep within where dreams and stories and visions appear. As Picasso noted, solitude is necessary for this work. In silence's calm surrounds, we discover the power of imagination and throw open the gates to creativity. In the opulent luxury of solitude, time becomes elastic and creative impulses surface and are allowed room to breathe. Sitting quietly, we gently enter our own inner worlds. Daydreaming. Woolgathering. Lost in space. These are rich and fertile activities. The playgrounds of imagination.

In *Amazing Grace*, Kathleen Norris writes about an exercise she devised for elementary school children regarding noise and silence. She told them that when she raised her hand, they could make all the noise they wanted to, and when she lowered her hand, they had to stop. The rules for silence were equally simple. When she raised her hand they had to sit and make no noise at all. Then they were to write about both experiences.

She writes, "What interests me most about my experiment is the way in which making silence liberated the imagination of so many children. Very few wrote with any originality about making noise. Most of their images were clichés such as 'we sound like a herd of elephants.' But silence was another matter: here, their images often had a depth and maturity that was unlike anything else they wrote. One boy came up with an image of strength as being 'as slow and silent as a tree,' another wrote that 'silence is me sleeping waiting to wake up. Silence is a tree spreading its branches to the sun.' In a parochial school, one third grader's poem turned into a prayer: 'Silence is spiders spinning their webs, it's like a silkworm making its silk. Lord, help me to know when to be silent.' And in a tiny town in western North Dakota a little girl offered a gem of spiritual wisdom that I find myself returning to when my life becomes too noisy and distractions overwhelm me: 'Silence reminds me to take my soul with me wherever I go.' "

Certainly the creative life can be filled with squalls and upheavals. Rejection, envy, fears, setbacks, even the heady and distracting pull of success and realized dreams are part of the meteorology we must ride out if we are to endure. But even coming to terms with loss, we need space to hear ourselves think, to sort out objectivity from personality.

And yet, even knowing this, I still forget.

I lose it without even knowing I've lost it. I fall into the habit of mindless listening. I overschedule my days. I cram meetings and phone calls around chores and daily writing. I wake up feeling cranky and out of grace and then I know it is time to withdraw again, to reconnect to the riches of time spent alone. To wrap myself in the stillness of the garden.

And so, again, I turn to silence to find myself. I turn to it so I can create.

CHAPTER 11

Conch Shell

Using Silence AS AN *Enhancement* TO *Health*

AFTER SPENDING only a week in her uncle's garden, Mary Lennox found that "she could run faster, and longer, and she could skip up to a hundred."

I also found that spending time in the garden of silence was paying dividends in terms of health. I was more relaxed. Less tense.

At a routine physical during the fifth year of my silent Mondays, my physician mentioned that my blood pressure reading was lower than it had been in the past. "What are you doing?" he asked. "Cutting out salt?"

"What am I doing?" I laughed. "Silence," I said. "I'm doing silence."

In the evening of each silent Monday, I was aware of being deeply rested. I felt restored both mentally and physically. I slept more soundly those nights.

This sense of well-being lasted into the week. At the same time, I was becoming more sensitive to excessive noise and growing less tolerant of the din to which we are daily subjected, at levels most of us accept as normal. I began to question them.

Conch Shell

At the movies, I found the sound level for trailers of upcoming films so assaultive I had to cover my ears. (Later, when I researched it, I learned that the audio for an action film operates at a level of 95–105 decibels, a range that extends from a chain saw to a jackhammer.) Theater employees usually refused requests to lower the sound, leaving two options: leave the movie or sit and suffer. At pop concerts the band amplification made it impossible to hear the singer. At a concert last summer the noise made my ears ring, a sign indicative of temporary hearing loss. And at a luncheon event I attended, the noise level in the restaurant was so high that I actually grew dizzy from the volume, another symptom of momentary hearing loss. It is telling that the root word for noise is "nausea."

A horticulturist once told me that houseplants respond to music. Heavy metal causes them to shrivel and become susceptible to disease. Surrounded by Bach and Beethoven, they flourish.

Are we less sensitive than a pot of English ivy?

In an essay penned in the early 1800s, Schopenhauer wrote, "Noise is becoming a threat to human health, and as such, ranks among the foremost environmental problems in the industrially developed countries." More recently,

William H. Stewart, the former U.S. Surgeon General, said, "Calling noise a nuisance is like calling smog an inconvenience."

Studies show that we are 46 percent more likely to have a heart attack if we live on a noisy street and 34 percent more likely if we work in a noisy environment. In addition to contributing to cardiovascular disease, high blood pressure, and higher serum cholesterol levels, noise has been linked to gastrointestinal problems, premature birth, lowered birth weight, immune suppression, and sleep disruption. And noise is a prime environmental cause of stress. Kierkegaard wrote, "The present state of the world and the whole of life is diseased. If I were a doctor and asked for my advice, I should reply, 'Create silence.'"

. . .

Hillary has experienced some hearing loss as a result of years spent around jet engines, whose decibel range is similar to that of air-raid sirens. Research shows some farmers experience noise-induced hearing loss by the age of thirty. Rock stars, too. Roger Daltrey of The Who is almost completely deaf. In Hong Kong, employees of mah-jongg parlors are now being compensated for hearing loss caused by the incessant, noisy clattering of the Bakelite tiles. Fans at hockey games often have temporary hearing loss, and if they are subjected to more noise, the loss is permanent. And according to a study done by Dr. Arlene Bronzaft for the New York City Council on the Environment, children who grow up in a particularly noisy environment are slower in cognitive language development.

Yet instead of lowering the volume to protect our hearing, our health, and our sanity, we jack it up.

Like so much about our bodies that we take for granted, our ears are both remarkably resilient and equally delicate. Within the inner ear is a spiral-shaped bone—shaped not unlike the chalky, sun-bleached conch shell that sits on my desk and reminds me to listen. This bone is the cochlea and it is lined with minute hair cells. Any sound creates a pressure wave that moves these hairs, which then transmit messages to the brain. High levels of noise damage these cells, and once damaged they cannot be repaired.

The *New York Times* recently reported that sounds of 85 decibels or more can cause damage if there is long or repeated exposure. A decibel (dB) is the unit used to measure sound, 0 dB being the minimum level needed to hear; 10 dB is the sound of a whisper or leaves blowing in the wind. Most of us are subjected to much greater levels, from which it is nearly impossible to escape. Studies show that 20 million or more Americans are daily exposed to racket that is permanently damaging their hearing. The *Times* article reported that measurements taken on seventeen subway platforms in the city showed that the mean maximum noise level was 94 decibels. In Union Square, the highest level was 106 decibels, again that of the sound of chain saws and jackhammers, as well as snowmobiles and rock music.

Are we like the frogs that, if put in a pot of hot water will jump out, but if put in a pot of lukewarm water that is gradually raised a degree at a time will boil to death? Do we lose our hearing a decibel at a time and not notice until we can no longer hear birdsong?

What happens then? As we unconsciously become desensitized in one area, do we begin to be unconscious in other areas? Do we fall out of touch with our world? And does this, in some way, make it easier to despoil that world?

. . .

Constant noise causes the neurons in our brains to shrink. The good news is that in a stress-free environment they will grow back. Our immune system is controlled by the vagus nerve, which runs from the brain and travels to all the important organs. Relaxation—calmness, peace, stillness—activates the vagus nerve and this activation boosts immune cell functions, reduces inflammation, helps prevent disease, and slows aging. Little wonder that meditation—the deliberate quieting of mind and body— has long been known to produce marked improvement in physical and psychological health. Since ancient times, it has been used to promote longevity and wellness. Now scientific research is showing that it actually makes our brains bigger and better.

"What do you gain by observing silence?" an acquaintance asked me one day.

"It makes me smarter," I said.

And it is not only to enhance health that we require silence. It is needed to help heal as well. When I had pneumonia several years ago, I craved stillness. If the bedroom became too noisy, my skin itched and I became agitated. Even the sounds of pots being set on the stove in the kitchen felt abrasive. It was as if an innate intelligence deep inside my body was urging me to seek quiet.

Every organ in our body has its own vibration. More and more body practitioners are incorporating sound healing, a means of getting a pitch at a certain vibration that mirrors that of the injured organ or tissue in spasm. This is work that must be done within a framework of silence.

.　　.　　.

Silence is needed not only to heal but to help us as we face the end of life.

My friend Dorothy Hebert took a vacation in England with her husband, Leon, who was very ill. While there, they visited a Peace Garden, one of several public parks throughout Great Britain where a rule of silence is imposed. These gardens, where the sick can go and sit in peace, were designed with the understanding of the role noise plays in fomenting disease and silence plays in healing.

When the couple returned to Illinois, Leon knew he was dying. He didn't want to watch TV, listen to the radio, or have friends visit. Concerned, Dorothy relayed this information to his doctor. Antidepressants were prescribed.

"Why?" Leon asked.

"Because the doctor thinks you're depressed," Dorothy said.

"Why does he think that?"

"I told him you didn't want to see anyone. Or even watch TV."

"I'm not depressed," Leon said. "I'm dying. Dying requires concentration. It requires quiet."

Living requires quiet, too.

It is so easy to forget this in our ever-noisy world. But over the years, on every other Monday, I would feel the truth of this in my body and psyche. I could hear the music of my breath, the rhythm of the blood in my veins, the wondrous gift of life in my own body.

Have you ever heard the sound of life inside your skin?

CHAPTER 12

Salt Marsh

Swimming into Deeper Waters

FOR SEVEN AND A HALF YEARS, I continued my rule of not speaking on the first and third Mondays of every month. Sometimes, I would float on the surface, resting and restoring. Other days, I allowed myself to go deeper, retreating into the depths and discovering more facets of myself and more lessons of silence. The only constant was that I never missed a day.

In October of the eighth year, I decided to devote an entire week to silence. I used an approaching book deadline as my "public" excuse for claiming a week of solitude, and I moved to our shorefront cottage.

The gray-shingled building sits at the end of a private dirt road fronting Nantucket Sound and overlooks a salt marsh. The bright blue door, an echo of the ocean's color, offers a cheery welcome. Walking into its pine-paneled space is like slipping into the past. There are four rooms as well as a glassed-in porch facing the sound. My father-in-law built this place in the 1940s as a simple summer home for his family. Simplicity is exactly what I was seeking when I arrived on that autumn morning. Simplicity, solitude, and silence.

Salt Marsh

The gulls in the marsh squawked and called as I carted the grocery bags up the back steps. I'd shopped earlier, buying enough food for three hearty meals each day, as if subconsciously overcompensating for the deprivation of companionship. After I finished unpacking the food, I stored the other supplies I'd brought, then dug out linens and made up the bed in the larger of the two bedrooms. In the living room, I set up my computer and placed the partially completed manuscript of my novel on the desk, but I was not yet ready to begin work.

I poured myself a small glass of sherry, put out a bowl of salted almonds, and touched a match to the kindling Hillary had set in the fireplace earlier. Although a radio and television were in the cottage, I was not tempted to turn them on. The crackling of the fire was music enough.

I sat in a wicker rocker, sipped the wine, and gazed out over the marsh. The grasses were losing their summer-green dress. Although I'd been anxious about meeting my approaching deadline, I suddenly felt relieved of all pressure. Three journals—left for summer tenants to write in—lay on the desk. I picked up the oldest, faded one and began to read.

"Bob White Cottage restoreth my soul," a man from Connecticut had written.

I hoped it would restoreth mine.

Earlier I'd told a friend about my plan to live by myself for a week in silence in this cottage by the sea.

"What are you going to do there?" she'd asked.

"I'll write. And probably do some reading."

"That's it?"

"I'll walk the beach. And sleep."

"A week alone. Without talking? Or company?" she'd said. "I'd go crazy. I'd be bored silly."

I didn't really know what to expect. A single day of silence was one thing, a full week something else entirely. Even on the most transforming of the days when I thought I'd gone deep, I suspected I had only waded at the edge of an ocean. Now I was heading out beyond the shoals. Alone.

A friend, learning of my Mondays and making the connection between silence and meditation, had sent me *The Miracle of Mindfulness*, by the Buddhist Zen master Thich Nhat Hanh, and now I recalled the line the author quoted from a Vietnamese folk song: "Hardest of all is to practice the Way at home, second in the crowd, and third in the pagoda."

So I wondered: As I swam into the waters of stillness and solitude with no family or friends on the horizon, would I be in over my head? Tossed by a sudden storm that rose from inside? Pulled out by a riptide? Or would I—as my friend put it—be bored silly?

The summer after our third wedding anniversary, Hillary and I had signed up to be a host family for the Fresh Air Fund. At the time, we were childless and were slightly anxious when Donald, an eight-year-old boy from Brooklyn, arrived. We muddled through the first days, finding our way. Donald was timid, nervous about the wooded lot next to our home, afraid that maybe bears lived in the "forest," and fearful, too, of the ocean, and refused to go barefoot at the beach. But gradually, day by day, he became less worried about his new surroundings and more comfortable with Hillary and me.

One day when it was raining and none of us wanted to play one more game of Candy Land, he sat looking out the window.

"Are you bored?" I asked, eager that he return to Brooklyn with happy memories of this time.

"What's that?" he said.

"Bored," I repeated, but he just looked puzzled.

How to define a word he had no concept of?

Bored.

I thought of my friend's reaction to the idea of my week here in silence and solitude. I recalled my own childhood and the hours I spent alone. Reading and riding my bike and investigating the woods and cornfields and the hayloft in the barn. Long minutes spent staring at clouds or cows. At what age, I wondered, do we develop a low tolerance for quiet time? When do we begin to call it boredom? When do we begin the excessive yearning for entertainment and diversions? The prospect of loneliness can make us fear solitude and silence. The paradox is that those are the very measures that can heal us.

·

While I was sitting, lost in memories of Donald and thinking of my friend's remark about my week alone, it had grown dark. I had no idea of the time. Again, I noticed how in silence, time often seemed elastic. Although I had not planned to do this, as if at the urging of the cottage I got up and unplugged the clocks in the bedrooms and kitchen. I removed my watch and placed it in the top drawer of a bureau.

This week I sought not only peace but release from the artificial constraints of man-made time. I wanted freedom from the tyranny of the telephone and the habit of clock-watching that produced another kind of mind chatter. I wanted to experience the fullness of silence, the expansiveness of it. I sought the secret pleasure of sitting in a closed-in garden. For this week I would live by my internal timepiece, eating when I was hungry, sleeping when I needed rest, keeping track of passing hours only by the ebb of the tidal flow in the marsh and the passage of the sun across the sky.

I thought about the distant summers my husband's family spent here when the only entertainment was provided by books, card games, and croquet. I thought of *their* ancestors and a long-ago time when the artifice of clocks and watches was nonexistent, when the sun and moon and clouds served as guides and anchors. Was my week here a bridge to the past, or a basic urge to tune my soul to nature's time and rhythm?

What creatures of habit we are. The first thing I did when I woke in the morning was to turn to the bedside table and check the clock. Its face was blank, the digital readout erased. I felt like a schoolchild on vacation. I stretched and rolled over, staring at the ceiling, lost in daydreams, and then slipped back into sleep. When I woke, the cottage was flooded with sun.

Still in my nightgown, I took my coffee outside and sat

on the deck, my feet propped on the porch rail. The tide
flooded the marsh, creating islands of the uplands. A red-
wing blackbird flew among the reeds, perched on a catkin,
near a broom cranberry bush. A heron, one of the flock
of seven living on the hillock in the middle of the marsh,
soared and landed. I watched as he stood, regal and motion-
less, showing me how to be still. How to be.

. . .

Spontaneity seemed to be the only order of my day. For
breakfast I had an orange, and then, though it was early
October, I decided to go swimming. I changed into a swim-
suit and headed down a narrow path through the marsh,
past an autumn olive tree, shortened and bent near horizontal, a bonsai pruned by salt winds. I crossed over the
rickety wood bridge spanning the clam flat that ran along
the south edge of the marsh.

The waters of Nantucket Sound still held summer's
warmth. I swam and floated and played in the ocean until
my fingertips shriveled. If I had been my child, I would have
ordered myself back on land. My hair, unconfined by a cap
or clips, floated in the sea around me. Water echoed in my
ears. I was utterly and totally free. Deeply at peace.

Later, back at the cottage, I stripped and ran from the

rear door to the outside shower wearing nothing but a towel. Naked as a bluejay, my grandmother would have said. In fact, at the very moment a bluejay was watching me from his perch on a branch of a nearby juniper. The sun warmed my body. The air stroked my skin. Bliss, I decided, would be showering outside for the rest of my life.

Do you have rituals you perform each day in the care of your home and body, acts you perform mindlessly, your attention already on what you will be doing next? Undergone mindfully, they can become small rites. Attention is a form of prayer, or at least the first prerequisite. Something as ordinary as bathing can become an ablution. My shower under the sky felt like that.

Finally I sat down to write. Silence surrounded and penetrated me. The world outside the cottage receded. In the quiet, I heard the soft voice of inspiration. Only the encroaching dusk and the marsh, flooding with water as the tide again reversed, told me that hours had passed.

That evening, I ate dinner by candlelight, as if even light cast by an electric lamp would prove too harsh. In silence, everything was softened and called out for more softness. I had thought I might miss music, but I didn't. At least not yet. Like Emily Dickinson, I had developed "the appetite for silence."

Before I slept that night, released from peripheral concerns, I heard the longings of my own heart. In stillness I had time to ponder, to bring up the treasures of the day. Without the distractions of everyday life, silence opened a space for me to converse with the deepest parts of myself. I paid attention to the thoughts that arose. I observed the hopes and dreams, the aspirations, fears, and visions I held inside. I felt so privileged to know an entire week of this lay ahead.

By Wednesday I was enormously rested. After breakfast I left the cottage and headed toward the beach. Writing awaited, but I wanted to take advantage of the last glorious days of Indian summer. Soon it would be too cold to walk barefoot, to swim in the sound. I returned to the wooden bridge, where I stared out at the marsh, banking what remained of summer's joys.

Salt marshes develop in quiet waters. Scientists tell us that they play a critical role in the Cape's ecosystem. They serve as nurseries for a number of fish and animal species, are buffers against coastal storms, and function as filters for nutrients flowing back into coastal waters from septic systems and animal waste. Ecologists warn that the salt marshes along the East Coast are dying and blame the impact of the overharvesting of natural predators of snails and crabs, which results in the death of key marsh grasses, as well as global warming and the effects of increased development along the fragile shore areas.

As I looked out over the marsh, sorrow swept through me at the thought of this living ecosystem dying. I wished a healing for it, just as silence was healing my own soul. Then I sat and listened, enraptured by the muted sounds of nature: bees and crickets, water lapping at the shore, the harsh cries of crows and gulls. I thought of Rumi's admonition: "Observe the wonders as they occur around you. Don't claim them. Feel the artistry moving through, and be silent."

Gradually I was aware of other sounds. The drone of a plane overhead. A car door slamming. Two voices carrying over from the beach parking lot. Something petulant was in the woman's voice, as if she was always asking for something. I was resentful of these noises—too harsh, intrusive, and demanding. I did not welcome them as connectors to humanity. I shut them out to concentrate on the natural world. To hear the whispers that are life in the tidal marsh.

It was slack tide, the interval between high and low tides when water lies still, not moving, like that brief cessation of breath, that moment of no breath at the end of an exhalation and before an inhalation.

Silence was my own slack tide. A natural stillness in the cycle of hours and days. I couldn't remember when I had felt such peace. I was honoring a deep rhythm, both personal and universal. One second melted into the next, one minute flowed to another, all of time one effortless continuum, suspended. There was a correlation, I thought, between silence and timelessness. Both breed a cessation of urgency.

The day itself felt like a poem.

I had no idea how long I sat. Only that I was no longer aware of anything but the marsh, as if I had *become* the marsh—the sand fleas in the dune behind me, the clams and fiddler crabs in the mud of the flat, the voles and shrews and caterpillars in the grasses, the breeze in the reeds. And then, as if my body was a fork tuned to the same vibration, I felt a transcendent unity.

In *Teaching a Stone to Talk*, Annie Dillard wrote, "You empty yourself and wait, listening. After a time you hear it: There is nothing there. . . . You feel the world's word as a tension, a hum, a single chorused note everywhere the same. This is it: This hum is the silence."

As I sat on the bridge I heard it: The "single chorused note everywhere the same." The hum of silence.

· · · ·

The week passed. Some nights I heard the mournful call of an owl, the howls of coyotes somewhere nearby, the wind stirring in the trees, whistling over the chimney, making the cottage creak like an old rocking chair. One day it rained and I listened to little staccato notes on the roof, like rice thrown against a window. I had not felt this directly connected to nature since I was a child. In silence, a part of myself that had been deeply asleep was waking.

I grew most restless at mealtimes. To eat with nothing external drawing attention felt odd. Usually when I ate alone I also watched television or read. Now I felt as if I were tasting food for the first time. The store of groceries I'd carried in were barely touched, as I simplified even that aspect of my days. I discovered it was harder to gulp food when there was nothing to distract, so I ate more slowly and was satisfied with less. I had a piece of fruit for breakfast. Or a boiled egg. Lunch and dinner were pared down, too. A salad and ear of corn. A dish of cereal topped with fresh berries.

I was reminded of an exercise recommended by the monk Thich Nhat Hanh. Take eight minutes to eat an orange. Take two minutes to eat a raisin. Really. Two minutes. He maintains that only then can we really taste its essence, see the universe it contains. Can you imagine? If you are at all like me, chances are you can down a raisin in four seconds.

I ate an apple slowly, counting neither minutes nor bites, trying to taste the world it held. The skin gave way beneath my teeth. The slightly grainy pulp sat on my tongue. Juice ran down my chin. I pictured the tree, the branch that had held it, the hard, brown seed it sprang from, the delicately tinted blossom it once had been, the sun that had warmed it, the land and water that had nourished it, the farmer who had picked it, the long and timeless story this one small fruit held. Never had I eaten with such focus and attention.

Not until Saturday morning was I overcome with a sense of loneliness, an isolation that gave into sadness. I missed Hillary and Hope and Chris. I missed talking and laughing with my friends. Again I thought of the Vietnamese folk song. "Hardest of all is to practice the Way at home . . ." I considered cutting my stay short by a day. Pride alone kept me from packing. I imagined reactions to my early return. *What? You can't stay by yourself for a week? So this silence practice isn't so great after all?* Instead, I headed again for the bridge that spanned the clam flat. The sounds of the salt marsh, so familiar, enfolded me. Gradually, melancholy eased.

I stepped lightly as I approached the flat, but the vibrations of my footfalls alerted a herd of fiddler crabs. Waving their oversized claws, they sidled and scuttled into burrows in the wet sand.

A blue box kite appeared overhead, its long tail trailing out, like calligraphy inked on the sky. Voices wafted over from the beach. A child laughing. An easy laugh. Two boys calling out in boisterous play. I smiled at the sound of these lovely human voices.

"The best remedy for those who are afraid, lonely, or unhappy," Anne Frank wrote more than half a century ago, "is to go outside, somewhere where they can be quite alone with the heavens, nature, and God."

How did one so young, imprisoned in an attic, become so wise?

I wept at the bittersweetness of life.

On Sunday I packed my belongings and prepared to leave. I was stronger than when I'd arrived seven days before. This had been a retreat, not from life but to live more fully in it. To reach deeper into my work. To learn more fully who I was. And who I had been as a child when I had felt most connected to nature.

But something else had happened. Each day I'd had the growing sense that I was part of something beyond myself.

There had been a presence with me, around me during

the week. I'd felt it as I'd walked the beach, sat on the wooden bridge, communed with herons and sand fleas and salt-marsh caterpillars, witnessed the ebb and flow of the tides, showered under the sun, watched the moon rise over the marsh. I was not ready to put a name to it. Nor was I ready to talk about it. In truth, it both brought me peace and scared the knickers off me.

For more than seven years I'd waded at the edges of silence. Now, swimming into deeper waters, I had a taste of what I had been seeking.

I felt the pull of it. And an equal measure of resistance.

PART FOUR

Harvest

CHAPTER 13

Lone Oak

From Speechlessness
TO *Solitude*

IN THE DAYS FOLLOWING my return home from Bob White Cottage, I thought a great deal about how much I had enjoyed being alone. My desire for peace and personal space intensified, as if that one week had whetted my hunger for more. I yearned both for silence and for its companion: solitude. This longing went deep, to a degree that I found unsettling.

Once, my friend Betty told me that in the early days of her marriage she would spend hours in her photography darkroom and never want to come out. She confessed she had found this urge unnerving. *What does this mean?* she'd wondered at the time. *Am I going crazy?*

Like Betty, I had troubling questions: Were my silent days turning me into a hermit? Was I slipping into some weird depression? What were the implications of this awakened appetite for seclusion? Did it reveal unacknowledged issues in my relationship with Hillary? Was I running from responsibilities? From my marriage? Should a "happily married" woman have such an intense craving for solitude? What effect would a pulling back, a pulling in, have on my family life? Could I fulfill this desire within the bounds of my normal life or—disturbing thought— was this the first ripple that would lead to a seismic shift? I knew the cautionary stories: the woman who came to Cape Cod for a summer alone and never returned to her family; the couples whose separate vacations morphed into separate lives.

In spite of the examples of philosophers, theologians, and pilgrims showing us that solitude engenders our strengths, despite the enforced solitudes of Gandhi, Nelson Mandela, and Martin Luther King Jr., experiences that changed not only their personal histories but social and political histories as well, we harbor self-generated fears that to be alone means we will be isolated, separate, excluded. Lonely.

I shared my concerns with Margaret.

"Maybe it simply means that you need to carve out more time alone," she said.

"But I work all day alone. Shouldn't that be enough?"

"Apparently not," she said, adding, "I don't think there are rules and timelines for soul desires."

"We must re-learn how to be alone," Anne Morrow Lindbergh wrote. And I was learning.

On the next silent Monday, in November, I returned to Bob White Cottage. The sky was leaden gray, forecasting the days ahead as autumn edged into winter. I'd come to shut the cottage down, but I was reluctant to begin. Each chore—storing window screens, taking down curtains, removing slipcovers from the cushions of the wicker chairs—signaled the end of my favorite season.

Mid-morning, I paused in my work, poured coffee in a cobalt blue mug, and went out to the deck. If I needed another reminder of what was to come, the salt marsh reflected it as clearly as a calendar. The reeds and grasses had faded from green to dull yellow.

I pictured creatures, hidden from my sight, going about their own preparations for winter, nature's equivalent to draining pipes and storing string hammocks. A line from Ecclesiastes popped into my head: *To everything there is a season, and a time to every purpose under the heaven.* I've always been drawn to that verse. Not only for the beautiful cadence of its rhythm, but for its timeless and comforting sense of the rightness of seasons.

What would happen, I wondered, if, like the animals and insects of the marsh, we were able to be entirely present to each day instead of regretting the loss of those past or anticipating those to come? What if we were completely present to each hour, each minute?

As I looked over at the hummock rising from the grasses to the east, a great blue heron crested. I knew that the hummock was home to a family of them. I had seen fox there, too. And, once, a deer. According to a surveyor's map dating from the 1930s, this is Ebenezer Weeks Island. On the northernmost tip, a single oak stands apart.

Hillary once told me trees growing in a forest are fundamentally weaker and less able to weather wind and storms than ones that stand alone, because the solitary trees, without the shelter provided by the others, develop stronger, deeper roots.

Staring at the oak, I remembered Hillary's words and considered the possibility that my desire for solitude represented not a weakness but a wish to grow stronger, not a running away from family and responsibilities but a running to myself, not a signal of something diseased in my life but of something healthy in my psyche. I thought again of the Bible verse, of the multitudinous seasons in life and the purpose of each.

What if, in the many seasons of my life, this was my season for solitude?

My season for solitude.

The phrase had a soft sound. Almost reassuring. As if a desire for solitude was a natural phase in one's life. A call to be not only heeded but honored.

I finished my coffee, and when I returned to work I imagined myself a marsh creature preparing for winter, in total harmony with the calendar of the universe. I pictured people and animals around the planet replaying these endless cycles for centuries. I remembered my mother setting the pressure cooker on the stove top. Its rack held a dozen Mason jars of stewed tomatoes, one batch of the scores of vegetables and fruits she put up for the coming season. I remembered my mother-in-law mulching the ground around rhododendrons against the winter freeze. I pictured squirrels burying acorns and quahogs burrowing deeper into the winter shoal, only to emerge in the spring. I thought of Thich Nhat Hanh's teachings that all things are inter-being.

In the weeks ahead, in that oddly synchronistic way that sometimes happens, as if we've tapped into a cosmic message board, I began receiving quotations about solitude. Although I had talked to no one except Margaret about my desire for time alone, quotes arrived like heat-seeking missiles. They came on the front of note cards and on calendar pages and on the leaves of books, each delineating the wisdom of, and our need for, solitude.

I began copying them in my journal. Two were:

Inside myself is a place where I live alone, and that's where you renew your spring that never dries up (Pearl Buck).

To develop our real selves, we need time alone for thought and meditation. To be always giving out and never pumping in, the well runs dry (Elizabeth Cady Stanton).

These authors, and others, understood how solitude could be a path to wholeness, to understanding, to ways in which we find healing and connection to all humanity. To the single humming note of the universe.

. . .

When I researched the etymology of "alone" I discovered it came from the Greek for "all-one." Was being alone, then, a way of being all one?

Since I had already carved out formal periods of silence, I decided to spend a large portion of each quiet Monday by myself. I had some concern that Hillary, Hope, and Chris might resent me pulling still further away and worried about how to balance the two seemingly disparate needs of achieving alone time and connecting with family and friends.

Eventually, I stopped agonizing over my desire for time apart and what it implied. Hadn't my silent days initially been met with resistance and curiosity, even judgment? And hadn't they proved to be enriching? Hadn't I learned that silence and solitude could strengthen my connection to others? Hadn't it been solitude and silence that taught Thomas Merton to love his brother monks?

So, as I had once committed to staying speechless on the first and third Mondays, I now dedicated part of those days to solitary time.

Alone, with my thoughts for company, I befriended my private self, all of me, my weaknesses and my fundamental worthiness. That was the challenge and the reward of alone time. In my garden plot of stillness and solitude, I reflected on matters of critical introspection that the pace and demands of modern life seldom allow time for. What do I believe? How do I want to spend the capital that is the time I am given on earth? What kind of partner am I to my husband; what kind of mother to my children? What is selfishness and what is self-care? What do I fear? What are my prejudices? How can I overcome them? What are my intentions? Like the lone oak tested by storms, I found that solitude was strengthening the roots of my personality and fertilizing the place where wisdom resides. And, like its sister, silence, solitude slowed me down.

I felt as if layers and layers of skin had been sloughed. I was moved to tears by things as simple as the sight of a hawk soaring overhead. Or the kindness of a stranger.

I would be derailed for long minutes, observing things that on an ordinary day I would brush right past. I was enthralled by squirrels leaping between the limbs of the oaks in our backyard, the interplay of baby chickens in the coop by our garage, the intricate beauty of a yellow and black spider on a windowsill.

These things not only pulled my attention but seemed infinitely worthy of consideration. Like a squatting child engrossed and enchanted by the activity in an anthill, I was mesmerized by life. And watching, I wondered, is there anything in nature that doesn't sit in itself, calmly?

I was beginning to explore what I was truly harvesting in my garden of silence.

Gradually, I slowed to a point below thought. Below questions. To a place of just being. To my childhood.

Long ago, before the dream of becoming a writer was a reality, I was being prepared for it. Like Rudyard Kipling, Anthony Trollope, P. G. Wodehouse, and Beatrix Potter, all of whom experienced isolated youths, I spent long hours quietly alone.

Our farm was on the outskirts of a small town. Both of my parents worked. There was one other child in the neighborhood, but, by the mysterious and carefully observed canons of childhood relationships, Janice could be playmate with either my older sister or me, never both at the same time. During those spells when she selected Sandy, I was on my own. Thus was I introduced to the richness of solitude.

In winter, I went sledding on the hill behind the far pasture or skating on the flooded surface of a swamp or a nearby pond. Spring, summer, and fall, I walked in the woods. Or played in the hayloft of the barn. Occasionally I hiked into the forest abutting our property, where I wrote secret messages on curls of white bark peeled from birch trees and left them for a stranger to discover, much like a child growing up by the seashore might slip a message in a bottle and heave it on the outgoing tide.

One of my favorite spots was out beyond the cornfields and hay pasture where my father kept the harrow, haymow, and wagon. Sunny afternoons I would mount a rusted metal seat, grasp imaginary reins in my fists, and pretend I was a cowgirl. I crossed prairies, had adventures, traversed horizons far beyond those of my circumscribed small-town life. There, in the unlimited territory of a young imagination, I made up movies where I got to be screenwriter, director, and star. And I never felt deprived.

But just as speech can both connect us or reinforce ego boundaries, so is it true of being alone. We can feel isolated or we can be freed to space beyond boundaries, to the openness of being. And because both solitude and loneliness imply being alone, we sometimes confuse solitude with isolation and rejection. The difference is that loneliness is often defined by lack. Solitude can be the instrument that connects us to ourselves and others.

Canyon Sam, a writer and performance artist from San Francisco, told me that during a twenty-day silent retreat in India she was sent away to spend time alone. From 5:00 a.m. to 10:00 p.m. she would alternately walk and sit in fifty-minute periods, stopping only for meals. Initially, she said, it felt like punishment. Although she was supposed to be meditating, she busied her mind by recalling the theme songs of television programs or advertising jingles, which she endlessly played in her head.

I wish I were an Oscar Meyer wiener . . .

See Ellis Brooks today for your Chevrolet . . .

One day toward the end of the retreat, as she walked around the pillars of the temple, instead of recalling jingles she posed a question: *What should I do when I leave this place?* The answer came immediately, as clear as the temple bells: *Love your parents.*

I can't do that, she thought. *They don't understand me. They don't support me.*

I'm running away from them. I'm disaffected. I can't go back.

In the final days, she kept repeating the question, kept checking. *Are you sure?* And the response was always the same: *Go home and love your parents.*

"In the abstract, 'Love all sentient beings' is easy," she said. "It's when applying it to the specific that we are tested."

When she returned home, Canyon followed the directive of the inner intelligence that had spoken to her alone in the shadow of the temple. Not long after, her father died, and the time she spent with her parents was the last period her father was in good health. And during their time together, Canyon discovered that her mother felt as disaffected as she did. They forged a new connection.

If Canyon hadn't been forced to spend time alone, would she have learned to love her family? Would she have heard the voice of her inner wisdom?

Lone Oak

An artists' colony is an interesting place to observe solitude and silence. On one hand it is set up to allow for exactly that. Contrarily, there are plenty of opportunities for lively interaction among the residents.

For many years each spring, I have spent four to six weeks at the Virginia Center for the Creative Arts. After a day working in solitude in the individual studios, dinner is a time of coming together, a social event where the artists and composers and writers gather in the communal dining room. Conversation is usually stimulating and loud, often overpoweringly so, as the fellows debate politics, exchange life stories, offer support for work gone awry, and make plans for after-dinner ping-pong games or open studios.

One spring in my ninth year of silence, while I was at the VCCA, the birthday of one of the visual artists fell on my silent Monday. At the end of the meal, the chef came into the dining room with a birthday cake bearing lit candles. The other twenty-three residents began singing "Happy Birthday" and a sense of festivity and play filled the room. As I sat, suddenly and unexpectedly, I felt the pain of exclusion, of being the only girl in the fifth grade not invited to the party. As consolation, I reminded myself that the others weren't deliberately leaving me out, that it was my choice to be silent, that in fact they weren't even aware of how sad I was feeling. But still I felt excluded. I was the Other.

I reasoned that I was being ridiculous, but thinking this did not make the feeling disappear or even ease. My sadness grew, as if this moment had tapped into every past moment of rejection. Finally as the song ended, I slipped away from the dining room.

The long driveway from the residence hall winds down to the main road and curves through meadows where a local dairy farmer pastures his herd. As I walked down to the gate, I felt their unblinking cow-gaze on me. The sense of isolation abated. Within the space of a few minutes, I was able to reflect on what had occurred back in the dining hall. Although the other residents had not deliberately—or even consciously—excluded me, for those few moments I had known what it felt like to be an outsider. And I understood that it is exactly the pain of that experience that makes us resist solitude.

And then I realized what a gift it had been to feel excluded, to experience the hurt of being left out. Of being in the minority. There are some lessons that are most powerfully learned when they are experienced viscerally, and this was one. This time the gift of silence taught me not to exclude others out of thoughtlessness or prejudice or insecurity or my own ego's need to feel superior. In seventeen years of practicing silence, it has been one of the seminal lessons.

Within the sphere of solitude and silence, we hear the voice of wisdom. It tempers us and strengthens us just as the winds make the lone oak more durable.

As Picasso said, "Without great solitude no serious work is possible."

Serious work, I think, of the soul as well as the canvas.

CHAPTER 14

Archer's Bow

Moving through Resistance

THE SENSE that silence was deepening and leading me to unfamiliar ground had been growing since the week at Bob White Cottage. But mostly, I didn't think about this. I took it a day at a time, open to whatever came.

And then, early one Monday in January of the ninth year, I woke and flat out wanted to quit.

In the past, there had been Mondays when, because of pressing obligations, silence had been inconvenient. Days when I'd had to adjust a writing workshop or a book tour schedule to accommodate my practice. Times when I had to travel. Or when we'd had overnight guests. And there were months when holidays and celebrations fell on a first or third Monday (Labor Day, July Fourth, New Year's Eve, my birthday, Hope's birthday). Yet, in spite of all these challenges, I'd kept my vow.

There were also times when the contrast between regular life and stillness was particularly jarring, days when silence seemed too stark compared to the racket of ordinary life, the quiet unsettling. On these days, I had to edge into my practice. I'd still keep to the one inviolate rule of nonspeech, but I'd put music on the CD player or watch the morning news for a half hour, weaning myself step by step from the outer world into one of stillness. Usually those were the days I most needed to be quiet. The busyness of my life had pulled me far off center. As if I'd misplaced the key to the gate that guarded my garden.

My reaction this morning felt different. I really didn't want to have an entire day of not speaking. Sushi, in winter-cat mode, curled tight against my side. I stroked her belly and stared up through the skylight at the pale heavens, weighed by an inertia that kept me from rising. Questions buzzed as persistent and troubling as biting gnats. *Why am I doing this? What am I trying to prove? Has this become an exercise of ego, proving I'm different, special, enlightened? Why not just stop?*

.   .   .

In truth, despite the many benefits—the restoration, the increased creativity, the strengthening of self—nine years seemed enough. That's all. The novelty had long ago worn off. Perhaps I'd grown weary of introspection. Of witnessing what arose each time. Of facing my compulsions and obsessions and prejudices. Of surrendering control. Of willingly withdrawing from the broad and familiar path of daily life. Of dedicating two days every month, year after year, regardless of what was going on in the world and in my corner of it. Or did it just seem this way? And what were my true reasons for practicing anyway?

I thought about the opening line in "The Three Silences of Molinos," a poem Henry Wadsworth Longfellow had written to John Greenleaf Whittier.

Three Silences there are: the first of speech,
The second of desire, the third of thought

In the past nine years I, too, had come to know several levels of silence. The first was easy silence, the kind that happened without conscious thought or intention. Moments when I'd find myself alone in nature, or in a quiet room, drifting off, daydreaming. The next level was deliberate silence, the purposeful stillness when I chose not to speak or to call in extraneous noise, a peacefulness that often led to a contemplative silence, one that was revealing and centering. The deepest level and most transformative was a profound transcendence. Not without thought but beneath thought.

Now I was tired of it all. Wasn't the garden completely explored, its soil exhausted? Or was I just feeling rebellious? Like a child feigning a stomachache to get out of school, I tried to think of an excuse that would let me off the hook. But let off the hook by whom? There was no one I had to answer to. No one was making me keep silence.

The battle, of course, was within.

The idea of stopping both relieved me and made me feel strangely guilty. Almost sad. Finally, as I had done that long-ago day on my third Monday of silence, I struck a bargain with myself. I vowed to continue for two more months and then, if I still wanted to quit, I would.

The matter settled—at least for the moment—I showered, dressed, and headed down to the kitchen. I didn't turn on the television. Whatever was going on, the solution wasn't to add noise. And I didn't feel anxious or in need of diversion. It wasn't as if I needed to talk, or phone a friend, or head out to shop. I just wanted to be relieved of silence. Done with it.

I made coffee and fed Sushi. Poached an egg. Ate. Did the dishes. Folded newspapers. Straightened the house. Took out the trash. Put a load of laundry in the washing machine. Brought order to my external life. And then, as I always do when I need to reflect and sort things out, I walked to the shore.

· · ·

For days we had been experiencing a spell of cold weather, temperatures stuck in the mid-teens, which was unusual for Cape Cod. Because of the ocean's tempering effect, our winters are usually mild. That day, a crusty, rippled covering of ice stretched several yards out into Nantucket Sound. Underfoot, the frozen sand crunched.

The wind blew nearly horizontal. Overhead, a small plane flew by, heading toward Nantucket, the sun winking on its wings.

When I was getting my pilot's license, the most difficult maneuver for me to master was crosswind landings. I used to dread practicing them. Unlike upwind landings, when the plane's nose heads straight down the runway on approach, in crosswinds the nose is turned into the wind until just before touchdown. Approaching a landing strip with the propeller facing off center felt alien and against all my instincts. While fighting my inclination to straighten out the plane, I also had to set up a wing-down or slip correction position, which means lowering the upwind wing and holding the opposite rudder. Since the Chatham airfield has a single landing strip laid east to west and the prevailing winds are southwest, I was given plenty of opportunities to confront my own resistance to crosswind landings.

Each time, wind was the enemy. I'd tense on the approach and grow sweaty.

"Don't fight it," my instructor, Bob, would say.

"Right," I'd manage as my hands tightened on the controls.

"Relax," he'd say. "Make the wind work for you."

I wanted to shoot him. As soon as we were back on the ground.

And then one day, I stopped struggling and just flew the plane. It wasn't anything Bob did or said, or any conscious attitude adjustment on my part. It just happened. I felt as if the wind and plane were partners. It required attention, of course. But that was all. I had only to pay attention. And to let go of fear.

Was resistance, then, based in fear?

But why should I fear silence now?

Hadn't it become my friend and teacher?

What was happening?

In the past, on silent days, of course I'd had to sit in sorrow, my heart uneasy. And eventually silence would soften and heal me. I'd sat in impatience and been led to patience. I'd reflected on words spoken foolishly or thoughtlessly and learned to be still, to wait for the deeper wisdom that lies beneath words. Was I now to explore resistance and see what it held for me? Where, exactly, did the resistance lie?

I thought, with some exhaustion, it's when the gloss of novelty wears off that the practice truly begins.

Years before, when I was taking a weekly yoga class, I hit a spell when I not only felt as if I wasn't progressing but as if I were actually becoming less flexible, possessing less stamina. I'd come out of even the least demanding asanas to rest in child's pose. This went on for several weeks and, discouraged, I mentioned it to my yoga instructor. Don encouraged me to be gentle with myself. Stay with it, he advised. Let go of judgments and expectations. His response frustrated me. It was too Zen. Wasn't practice supposed to improve your ability, build strength and stamina? It certainly shouldn't make you go backward.

Then, one week later, I surprised myself by easily holding a difficult variation of *Trikonasana*, the triangle, a pose I had always struggled with in the past. At the end of class, I approached Don. "Isn't it odd," I said. "For weeks I've felt so stiff and inflexible and now suddenly I can do this pose?"

He smiled. "Sometimes we have a period that looks like a setback," he told me, "but in reality that time is a place of preparation. A resting space. A gathering of energy. Like an archer pulling back the bowstring so the arrow can shoot forward."

The analogy made sense.

I reflected on Don's words as I walked along the winter beach. New questions arose. Could my resistance be not fear but simply a resting place? A gathering place? Preparation? But a readying for what?

CHAPTER 15

Lily Pad

Considering Spirituality

IN THE FOLLOWING two months, I continued observing silence.

Some days I feared it was leading me to a scary place away from the garden. Other days I was reluctant to let go of this refuge of peace and healing.

One day, wanting a change of scenery, I headed over to the town of Brewster on the Cape's north side. I drove to an old gristmill that sits by a herring run. I parked, grabbed a bottle of water, and crossed the street to the upper pond, one of the hundreds that formed when the great sheets of ice that once covered the Cape melted.

For a while I walked the perimeter, but before long, lulled by the sun's warmth on my shoulders, I found a spot to sit. Around me, the place was alive with activity. Birds darted overhead; bugs buzzed in the grasses; green, lacy-winged dragonflies skimmed over the pond surface. A few feet out, a frog, as sun-stunned as I, basked on the wide waxy leaf of a lily pad. Several of the lilies were in blossom, their white petals catching and reflecting light and awakening old memories.

Lily Pad

During the first two years of our marriage, we used to rent out our home each summer and move to a cabin Hillary had built deep in the woods on the edge of a pond much like this one. We dubbed the eighteen-by-twelve-foot cabin the Honeymoon Hut. A single room, it contained a bed, a bureau, two wooden chairs, a sink and hand pump, a gas stove and gas-fueled refrigerator, and one small pine table where we ate our meals and played cards into the evening by the light of a kerosene lantern.

Occasionally, Hillary would take our kayak, paddle out to the center of the pond, and cut a lily blossom for our table. I thought it the most romantic of gestures. Throughout those nights, lily fragrance would perfume the cabin. One day, when Hillary was at work, I set out in the kayak, but when I reached the grouping of pads I realized I had forgotten to bring a knife. Determined to return with a blossom, I pulled and tugged on a thick, rubbery stem, but it would neither break nor be uprooted, and I returned to the cabin empty-handed. That evening, Hillary told me that although lilies appear to be just floating on the surface, their stems are buried deep in mud. I remember being struck by the visual contradiction of such a delicate, white blossom—the ancient symbol of purity—being rooted in dark mud, muck it held tight to.

We hold on to what feeds us.

Was this, then, why I was holding on to silence? Because it nourished me?

But what about my resistance? What was that rooted in?

Over the years, when people learned about my observation of silence, their most frequent reaction was a question: "Is this some kind of religious or spiritual thing?"

"No," I always replied quickly.

"Did someone suggest it, then?" they would ask. "How did you start?"

I'd say that it had been a whim, and, if people were still curious, I'd go on to explain how it had begun on the beach in a moment of gratitude.

"But why do you do it?" they'd ask.

I find it restful, restorative, I'd respond. It has taught me to listen. To pay attention. To reflect instead of react. I'd tell them it brought me back to myself.

But, no, I'd repeat, it wasn't a religious or spiritual practice.

It seems I was the last to know.

Hermits, saints, and mystics have always known silence is a powerfully meditative form of worship, one of the greatest single contributors to their spiritual growth. For centuries, silence and solitude have been central to religious traditions around the world, used to assist in the process of transformation. The Desert Fathers, fourth-century Christian hermits and ascetics, went alone into the wilderness of the Egyptian desert, hoping to find meaning through renunciation. Irish monks set out to sea alone in curraghs.

Today it is still a common custom for Hindus, both monks and laypeople, to set time aside each week for complete silence. In the West, the Society of Friends center their entire worship service around silence as a form of prayer. No dogma. No hierarchy. No sermon. Just sitting on wooden benches letting the spirit move, listening to what arises. Christian and Zen monasteries, convents, and Buddhist centers continue to offer refuge for those who are called to the cloistered life, but increasingly today they are also magnets for those seeking simplicity, serenity, and an escape from frenetic lives.

At many monasteries, the demand for these retreats is such that space often must be reserved a year in advance.

Reverend John D. Bavaro of the Franciscan Center in Andover, Massachusetts, recently told a reporter from *Time* magazine, "We're booked like we've never been booked before."

Perhaps we all need a gate to the garden where spirit can talk to us. And silence, by its very nature, provides this path.

So how had I not understood this? Why did I deny it?

For many years, I had felt distanced from the God of my childhood and disaffected with religion. The world around me buttressed this position: wars, political and personal, waged in the name of religion; institutions more concerned with filling their coffers than feeding souls; doctrines that seemed too proscribed and narrow; and battling factions, self-righteous and convinced of their truth, exclusive of all others. If this was religion, I wanted no part of it.

The idea of silence as a spiritual undertaking felt like a surrender I didn't want to make. I feared what it might mean. Where it might lead me. What I might be called upon to renounce.

And yet, stirrings persisted. I was drawn to explore varied spiritual traditions. To sort out my feelings about

religion and spirituality. I thought about how often we confuse them. I thought about how one is imposed from the
outside, the other from within.

My mind continued to question.

And my soul continued to seek.

·   ·   ·

The two months I had allowed myself passed, and I continued my silent Mondays. Like the pond lilies deeply rooted
in sediment, I seemed to need the nourishment that only
quiet provided.

I thought about my observation of silence over the
years. Each day it had asked only that I pay attention. It had
required only that I practice the art of listening.

And, Monday after Monday, through this steady, consis-
tent, mindful practice, I had come to find stillness, to listen
to the quiet voice within, to hear truth and tutor myself to
speak it with kindness. To give thanks. To offer respect. To
slow down and smell not only the flower by the roadside
and in the garden, but the compost that it once had been
and was again becoming. To open so I could receive rather
than resist. To be restored to the sacred rhythms of life.

Paying attention. Being in the moment of life. Honoring its sacred nature. In fact, realizing the ineffable, sacred nature of everything. Having reverence. If this is not the center of spirituality, then what is?

I thought about the number of times while in silence I had felt the presence of something around me, a sense so strong it could not be denied.

In *The Secret Garden*, Mary Lennox and, eventually, her cousin Colin found that something happened in the garden. They had no name for it and so they called it "the magic." It was as certain and as invisible as electricity.

I stopped searching for concrete answers to a mystery that transcended my comprehension.

And a gate opened.

One day, while working in my studio, I picked up the conch shell, fingered its intricate shell, its pearl-smooth, orange interior, held it to my ear. We are told we are hearing the ocean's echo, and seemingly do, but what we really hear is the sound of our own ears attuned.

I held the shell and thought of the Irish saying about the five-string harp.

Perhaps, in stillness, the tuning of four things—heart, mind, body, spirit—leads to the tuning of the fifth—the soul, which leads us to transcendence.

Lily Pad

When I began that January day seventeen years ago, I did not know why I was called to silence. I had no idea where it would lead me.

"Ah, yes," I answer now without a moment's hesitation, explanation, or apology. "My silence is a spiritual practice."

It has carried me home.

CHAPTER 16

September Beach

Preserving THE *Garden*

I WALK AGAIN to Nantucket Sound, to the beach where it began. Around me, the world stirs. And I, my five-stringed harp tuned and in harmony, open to its song.

The tide is low. A small flock of sea ducks and gulls feed just offshore in the lee of a rock jetty. The sky is blue and cloudless, just as on that afternoon years ago. But things are different now, too. Clumps of goldenrod bloom on the dunes and poison ivy leaves have turned bright scarlet. Lobster-red rose hips, as big as silver quarters, hang heavily from the branches of the *Rosa rugosas*. These bushes remind me of my father-in-law, who planted them there more than nearly three-quarters of a century ago. And of my mother-in-law, who taught me how to make jelly from the hips when I was a young bride. And these recollections remind me of the swiftness with which the years pass.

Like this beach, I, too, am both the same and changed.

I have thought a great deal about that long-ago day. What made me open to the idea of silence? Why was I receptive? Was it because I had reached an age and place—children older, career and marriage settled—that I could pause long enough in the course of an ordinary day to listen to its calling?

Often it takes a crisis or a catastrophe to jolt us from our daily routine, a catalyst that turns our lives upside down and forces us on a new journey not of our deciding. Death. War. Divorce. Disease. But there had been no exigency that day. Only sadness for the loss that Margaret would soon face when her mother died. And those few moments of gratitude as I stood transfixed, awake to the wonder of sea ducks feeding, to the world around me, aware, too, of the many blessings in my life. On the surface, an uneventful day no different from many others.

And yet . . .

I have read somewhere that there are three highways into the heart: Silence, Love, and Grief.

There is a fourth, too, I think. Gratitude. Which is a kind of love.

I see now that all four of these highways converged that day in me. In their way, they are as revolutionary as a crisis in claiming our attention.

.   .   .

Now, standing by the shore, I am as filled with awe and thankfulness as on that January afternoon. In this moment, I am sustained by a sense of wonder and peace, humbled by life, and respectful of it, connected to the planet and her people, and to something much greater than myself, an invisible essence for which I have no language. I live in its mystery, content to let it be revealed. I do not have to name it. It is enough to know its truth.

This is where silence has brought me.

I remember back to the first day and the two acquaintances who termed the idea of not speaking for a day radical. What a strange coincidence, I had thought at the time. Now I see it was not odd at all. In the truest sense, silence days have been radical, leading to the quietest of revolutions.

Silence has become such a part of me that I am able, almost on demand, to call up its peaceful state. I cannot imagine my life without these regular periods of stillness.

I know I am not yet finished with it.

Nor is silence done with me.

PART FIVE

Sowing

CHAPTER 17

Bridge

Crossing the Threshold to Silence

ON THE FIRST DAY of the workshops I lead on the practice of silence, all the participants express a great desire to incorporate stillness into their lives when they return home. We take long meditative walks in silence and together explore the many benefits of this practice. It is not until the final session, when we begin to get specific about how each will bring the practice into being, that resistance arises. One by one, my students articulate the specific difficulties of trying to carve out periods of silence. I write these responses on a large board, making a list I call the Guardians of the Gate. By focusing on the practical matters that reflect the group's projected fears, the list serves as a constructive way to look at resistance.

I have young children.

I have a demanding job and am already overscheduled.

I don't have any time for it.

My friends might think it is odd.

My family won't understand.

I am widowed and live alone. There is already too much silence in my life. The last thing I need is more.

When the list is finished, we begin brainstorming.

In one workshop, a counselor in a residential home for disturbed teenagers who is on call day and night explained, "People are in and out of my office all day long. Literally, the only time I am alone is when I'm sleeping."

"Let's start with this," I said. "Are you committed to finding a time for silence?"

"I am," she said. "I felt so calm yesterday morning on the walk. I know it's what I really need."

The group offered suggestions, trying to find a way the woman could incorporate stillness into her days, if only for a few minutes.

Finally one of the women asked, "Do you eat lunch?"

"Yes," the woman answered.

"Alone?"

"Usually."

"Could you close your door when you eat?" she asked. "Just have that time alone."

"I could," the woman said. Her voice grew excited. "I could put a sign on my office door saying 'Out to Lunch' and no one would even know I was still there."

I turned to the widow who lived alone. "How did you feel on the walk yesterday? Did it feel lonely or isolating not to talk? Did you miss conversation?"

She thought for a moment. "No," she said. "Actually, it was peaceful."

"Can you say why?"

She thought again and then laughed. "My attitude," she said.

"But what about young children?" a mother in the group asked.

"My experience is that children are intrigued by silence," I said. "If they're visiting on my Mondays, they often want to join me in not speaking."

The mother looked doubtful.

"Let me tell you a story about my mother," I said.

I told the group about my mother's experience one spring when she had an operation on her vocal cords. She taught in a primary school and for the entire last month of school she could not speak. When she needed to get the class's attention, she used a metal "Cricket" clicker. The students spoke in whispers. Behavioral problems disappeared. To this day, she maintains that in forty years of teaching, that was the quietest, most respectful class she ever had. Silence enriched her classroom.

Bridge

. . .

A Hindu monk wrote, "If I could get one percent of the world to practice silence, the world would be transformed."

And so we begin.

What will your secret garden look like? Will the space fill a field? An acre? A narrow border? Will you begin with an entire day? A weekend retreat? An hour before bed? Several minutes? The point is to begin to slow down your life and focus your attention.

. . .

Here are a few suggestions to start. Perhaps one will speak to you.

❖ On the commute to work or while running errands, turn off the car radio.

❖ When performing a routine chore—folding laundry, washing dishes, straightening a room, weeding the garden— make it a habit to do the task in silence.

❖ When a task is completed, sit in restful awareness for several minutes before running to the next chore on the list.

✣ After finishing a telephone conversation, sit quietly for a minute or two. Breathe.

✣ Take a long walk without earbuds pouring noise into your head.

✣ Proclaim one day a month, or one morning a month, a time of nonspeech. If an entire day or a half day feels too impossible, try an hour. Like a child learning to swim, wade in the waters of silence before swimming out.

✣ Break the habit of automatically turning on the radio or television when you walk into a room.

✣ Take the television out of your bedroom.

✣ Unplug the phone or turn off the ringer.

✣ Take a sabbatical from e-mail.

✣ When you are part of a group, experiment with just listening to the others converse, staying silent yourself. Observe your own inner dialogue.

There are, too, small gaps in our daily rounds where we can carve out moments of silence.

⚜ Waiting in line, in doctors' offices, in the car, sit without activity or without talking.

⚜ Have a meal alone. Without distractions. Without a book or magazine.

⚜ Arrange a vacation alone. A weekend or a week. Spend part of that time without talking, checking e-mail, or text messaging.

⚜ Enroll for a weekend at a retreat where silence is practiced.

⚜ Wake an hour early and spend that hour in deliberate stillness.

⚜ End the day in silence, an hour that will bring you back to yourself.

⚜ Tune your five-string harp. Awaken to your senses.

⚜ Set aside a formal silence time for your family.

⚜ Go to a place in nature and experience the peace. Walk along the seashore, take a mountain hike. In the movie *The Bucket List*, the two lead characters attempt a trek to the top of Mount Everest and one of them starts talking about how peacefully silent the summit is; how, if you are quiet enough, you can hear the mountain. (My friend Ilihia Gionson, who often goes to Mauna Kea on the Hawaiian island where he lives, says if you listen well, it doesn't take a mountain to speak to you.)

✢ Take five minutes and close your eyes, wherever you are.

✢ Watch birds. Look at trees.

✢ Watch the primrose or morning glory open. Be in awe.

✢ For one day, do things manually. Rake leaves instead of using a blower. Wash dishes by hand. Hang clothes rather than use the dryer.

✢ Stroke your cat.

✢ Keep a gratitude bowl of quotes about silence. Pick out one to meditate on for a day.

✢ Light a candle. Notice the moment when the fire meets the wick.

✢ Find a labyrinth to walk.

✢ Select a place of worship to visit in the middle of the day and sit for fifteen minutes.

✣ Go to the cemetery and clean the moss off your family's stone.

✣ Pack a picnic for one and lunch at a park or garden where you have never been.

There are many ways to sow the seeds. Listen and in the quiet you will hear the direction of your heart.

The garden of silence is always there for us.

Patiently waiting.

We have only to claim it.

Acknowledgments

THIS BOOK grew out of my journey of silence. Along the way, many people have supported and encouraged me, and I am indebted to them. To the following I am especially grateful. My thanks to:

☀ My agent, Deborah Schneider, who waves a magic wand over my work and blesses me with her friendship.

☀ Gail Winston, whose intelligence, generosity, and insight have made all the difference. Her wit has made it a pleasure. And special thanks to Sarah Whitman-Salkin and Shea O'Rourke, who have been ever available to answer my questions and respond patiently and graciously to even the most obtuse of them.

✢ The stellar team at HarperCollins. Special thanks to Leah Carlson-Stanisic.

✢ My son, Chris, whose photography so beautifully illustrates the spirit of silence.

✢ The Virginia Center for the Creative Arts and the Ragdale Foundation, which once again provided me with the necessary time and space to think and write. And thanks to the staffs of both centers, who welcome me home.

✢ Margaret and Stuart Moore, who gave me refuge in their Maine farmhouse when I most needed it.

✢ Ginny Riser, who read every page of the manuscript with the eye of an editor and the heart of a friend.

✢ Rose Conners, who read the manuscript twice and provided valuable input. And thanks, too, to the other two members of TBWGIWW: Mike Lee and Beth Seiser.

✢ All the friends who, over the years, so willingly shared their thoughts and experiences and support, sending quotes

Acknowledgments

and recommending books: Cleveland Morris, Canyon Sam, Susan Tillett, Dr. Christopher Leighton, Jebba Handley, Dr. John Clark, Judy Cornwell, Jackie Mitchard, Joan Anderson, Ann Stevens, Robert Reeves, Wayne Ferguson, Rev. Jim Robinson, North Cairn, Kathy Gottlicht, Shannon and John Tullius, Sam Horn, Ilihia Gionson, Wally and Ellen Winter, The Friends of Lake Forest, and Christine Askounis.

✢ To all those who have attended my silent workshops and retreats and have so generously shared their experiences and suggestions.

✢ And, as always, to my family—Hillary, Hope, and Chris—for the love that forms the foundation of my life.

Bibliography and Recommended Readings

Brady, Mark. *The Wisdom of Listening*. Boston: Wisdom Publishers, 2003.

Campbell, Eileen. *Silence and Solitude: Inspirations for Meditation and Spiritual Growth*. San Francisco: HarperSanFrancisco, 1994.

Cooper, David A. *Silence, Simplicity and Solitude: A Complete Guide to Spiritual Retreat*. Woodstock, Vt.: Skylight Paths Publishing, 1999.

Dillard, Annie. *Teaching a Stone to Talk*. New York: HarperPerennial, 1992.

Emoto, Masaru. *The Hidden Messages in Water*. Hillsboro, Ore.: Beyond Words Publishing, 2004.

France, Peter. *Hermits: The Insights of Solitude*. New York: St. Martin's Griffin, 1996.

Francis, John. *Planet Walker: How to Change Your World One Step at a Time*. Point Reyes Station, Calif.: Elephant Mountain Press, 2005.

Hanh, Thich Nhat. *The Miracle of Mindfulness*. Boston: Beacon Press, 1975.

———. *Being Peace*. Berkeley: Parallax Press, 1987.

———. *Peace Is Every Step*. New York: Bantam Books, 1991.

Judson, Sylvia Shaw. *The Quiet Eye*. Chicago: Regency Gateway, 1954.

Also recommended:

www.insilencetogether.com

www.listeningbelowthenoise.com

Bibliography

Lindbergh, Anne Morrow. *Gift from the Sea*. New York: Pantheon, 1955.

Kabat-Zinn, Jon. *Wherever You Go There You Are*. New York: Hyperion, 1994.

Kelly, Jack, and Marcia Kelly. *Sanctuaries: A Guide to Lodgings in Monasteries, Abbeys, and Retreats*. New York: Bell Tower, 1991.

Merker, Hannah. *Listening: Ways of Hearing in a Silent World*. Dallas: Southern Methodist University Press, 2000.

Merton, Thomas. *The Inner Experience: Notes on Contemplation*. San Francisco: HarperSanFrancisco, 2003.

Muller, Wayne. *Sabbath: Restoring the Sacred Rhythm of Rest*. New York: Bantam Books, 1999.

Norris, Kathleen. *The Cloister Walk*. New York: Riverhead Books, 1996.

———. *Amazing Grace: A Vocabulary of Faith*. New York: Riverhead Books, 1999.

Picard, Max. *The World of Silence*. Washington: Regenery Gateway, 1988.

Raine, Nancy Venable. *After Silence*. New York: Three Rivers Press, 1999.

Ram Dass. *Be Here Now*. New York: Harmony Books, 1971.

Storr, Anthony. *Solitude: A Return to the Self*. New York: The Free Press, 1988.

Taylor, Barbara Erakko. *Silence: Making the Journey to Inner Quiet*. Philadelphia: Innistree Press, 1997.

Watts, Alan. *The Way of Zen*. New York: Vintage, 1989.

Zukav, Gary. *Soul Stories*. New York: Simon and Schuster, 2000.

List of Plates

List of Plates

The images were taken with a digital EOS Canon Rebel XTI camera utilizing various zoom lenses.